AF606520

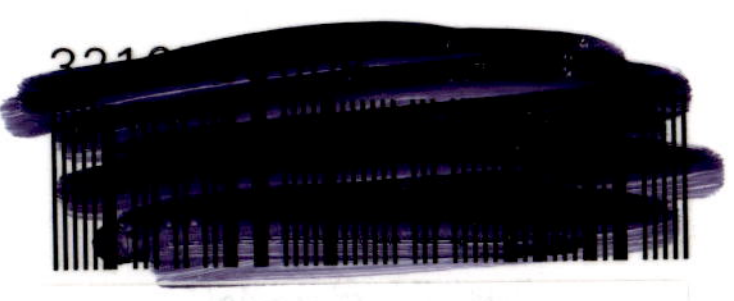

E-HEALTH: CURRENT STATUS AND FUTURE TRENDS

Studies in Health Technology and Informatics

This book series was started in 1990 to promote research conducted under the auspices of the EC programmes Advanced Informatics in Medicine (AIM) and Biomedical and Health Research (BHR), bioengineering branch. A driving aspect of international health informatics is that telecommunication technology, rehabilitative technology, intelligent home technology and many other components are moving together and form one integrated world of information and communication media.

The complete series has been accepted in Medline. In the future, the SHTI series will be available online.

Volume 106

Recently published in this series

Vol. 105. M. Duplaga, K. Zieliński and D. Ingram (Eds.), Transformation of Healthcare with Information Technologies
Vol. 104. R. Latifi (Ed.), Establishing Telemedicine in Developing Countries: From Inception to Implementation
Vol. 103. L. Bos, S. Laxminarayan and A. Marsh (Eds.), Medical and Care Compunetics 1
Vol. 102. D.M. Pisanelli (Ed.), Ontologies in Medicine
Vol. 101. K. Kaiser, S. Miksch and S.W. Tu (Eds.), Computer-based Support for Clinical Guidelines and Protocols – Proceedings of the Symposium on Computerized Guidelines and Protocols (CGP 2004)
Vol. 99. G. Riva, C. Botella, P. Légeron and G. Optale (Eds.), Cybertherapy – Internet and Virtual Reality as Assessment and Rehabilitation Tools for Clinical Psychology and Neuroscience
Vol. 98. J.D. Westwood, R.S. Haluck, H.M. Hoffman, G.T. Mogel, R. Phillips and R.A. Robb (Eds.), Medicine Meets Virtual Reality 12 – Building a Better You: The Next Tools for Medical Education, Diagnosis, and Care
Vol. 97. M. Nerlich and U. Schaechinger (Eds.), Integration of Health Telematics into Medical Practice
Vol. 96. B. Blobel and P. Pharow (Eds.), Advanced Health Telematics and Telemedicine – The Magdeburg Expert Summit Textbook
Vol. 95. R. Baud, M. Fieschi, P. Le Beux and P. Ruch (Eds.), The New Navigators: from Professionals to Patients – Proceedings of MIE2003
Vol. 94. J.D. Westwood, H.M. Hoffman, G.T. Mogel, R. Phillips, R.A. Robb and D. Stredney (Eds.), Medicine Meets Virtual Reality 11 – NextMed: Health Horizon
Vol. 93. F.H. Roger France, A. Hasman, E. De Clercq and G. De Moor (Eds.), E-Health in Belgium and in the Netherlands
Vol. 92. S. Krishna, E.A. Balas and S.A. Boren (Eds.), Information Technology Business Models for Quality Health Care: An EU/US Dialogue
Vol. 91. Th.B. Grivas (Ed.), Research into Spinal Deformities 4

ISSN 0926-9630

E-Health: Current Status and Future Trends

Edited by

George Demiris

Department of Health Management and Informatics, School of Medicine, University of Missouri-Columbia, USA

Amsterdam • Berlin • Oxford • Tokyo • Washington, DC

ISBN 1 58603 442 1
Library of Congress Control Number: 2004109510

Publisher
IOS Press
Nieuwe Hemweg 6B
1013 BG Amsterdam
The Netherlands
fax: +31 20 620 3419
e-mail: order@iospress.nl

Distributor in the UK and Ireland
IOS Press/Lavis Marketing
73 Lime Walk
Headington
Oxford OX3 7AD
England
fax: +44 1865 750079

Distributor in the USA and Canada
IOS Press, Inc.
4502 Rachael Manor Drive
Fairfax, VA 22032
USA
fax: +1 703 323 3668
e-mail: iosbooks@iospress.com

PRINTED IN THE NETHERLANDS

Preface

George DEMIRIS, PhD
University of Missouri-Columbia
USA

The concept of e-health introduces new channels of communication and transactions in healthcare and challenges the traditional definitions of patients' and providers' roles. E-health is often viewed as the digital transformation of care delivery and redesign of the business models that prevail in the health care industry. For the purposes of this book, we define e-health as the use of advanced telecommunications such as the Internet, portable and other sophisticated devices, advanced networks and new design approaches aiming to support healthcare delivery and education. Thus, e-health refers to a fundamental redesign of healthcare processes based on the use and integration of electronic communication at all levels. It aims to lead to patient empowerment which describes the transition from a passive role where the patient is the recipient of care services to an active role where the patient is informed, has choices and is involved in the decision making process.

Within the context of e-health, the term "consumer health informatics" is often used to describe the study of behaviors and information seeking patterns of patients in their role as consumers of health related information and managers of their health decisions. Obviously, the Internet has played a great role in enabling consumers to access a wealth of information and exchange knowledge with peers and support groups. However, other advanced technologies have also introduced innovative ways of empowering patients and improving the patient-provider communication. Technological advances such as wearable devices and sensors that capture and automatically transmit vital signs, mobile applications that enhance care delivery and enable disease prevention or early detection and new applications of electronic medical records are emerging. In addition to the evaluation of the impact of such applications on the health status of citizens, we need to address issues related to policy and reimbursement and furthermore, create an ethical framework for the design and implementation of such systems. The ethical issues are also an integral part of research in the era of post-genomic medicine.

E-health has the potential to improve efficiency on a global level when patients cross national boundaries to seek treatment in other countries and to enable medical facilities and services across countries to be linked and accessible to citizens. This book is the result of a two-day conference that took place in February of 2004 in Columbia, Missouri. The conference was sponsored by the European Union Center of the University of Missouri-Columbia and the Department of Health Management and Informatics and examined issues of e-health applications in the United States and Europe. Guest speakers from Europe and the US covered a broad range of e-health issues and carried out a dialogue between researchers, practitioners, vendors and consumers. Discussion topics focused on the use of mobile technologies in health care, "smart home" technologies, telemedicine applications that cross national borders, transatlantic collaborations in bioinformatics and the use of the Internet in health care. Furthermore, legislative efforts and ethical concerns associated with the diffusion of e-health were discussed and policies in the EU and the US were reviewed and compared.

This book reflects the discussion that was fostered by the conference and covers a wide range of topics related to e-health research. The contributors are academic researchers from the European Union and the United States and are presenting current work, future trends and a discussion of challenges that will arise in the coming years.

The concept of telemedicine is obviously an essential component of the e-health era. Hicks and Boles present a model that provides a systematic framework to be used in evaluating the effectiveness, efficiency, and feasibility of telemedicine. Demiris describes telehomecare and smart home applications and provides an overview of an evaluation framework for home-based e-health applications and the associated implementation challenges.

E-health will have a great effect on medical education. Headrick describes the qualities required for future physicians to deliver the care that their patients need and deserve, in the context of e-health. There are professions that might have been traditionally not included in the digital transformation of medicine that can benefit from the use of new technologies. Oliver and Demiris discuss the potential application of e-health tools for social workers. The use of such tools impacts the way health care professionals and researchers conduct their work. Patrick et al address the issue of standards for information retrieval to support decision making in e-health.

Contributors of this book also discuss innovative technologies and new concepts that are being introduced by e-health. Schopp discusses the concept of telework for people with disabilities and provides a comparison of the current status in the United States and Europe. Mitchell explores ways that the Human Genome Project will change health care and she also investigates the ways that e-health systems will be influenced by the genomic data. De Moor and Claerhout highlight the relevance of privacy enhancing techniques in the context of e-health. Chan defines and discusses health captology, the application of persuasive technology to health care, and its potential to leverage proven persuasive techniques to improve clinical outcomes.

Finally, specific projects that are currently being carried out and demonstrate future trends, are being described. Van Halteren et al. describe the MobiHealth system which is based on the concept of a Body Area Network (BAN) allowing high personalization of the monitored signals and thus adaptation to different classes of patients. The system and service have been tested in four European countries. Pinciroli et al provide a description of an audible web-based medical record for emergency patients and in a different chapter discuss service level web monitoring in the field management of emergencies. Pedersen provides an overview of e-health in the Nordic countries and the way the national health care system of a country impacts the diffusion rate of e-health.

I would like to thank all of the contributors of this book. I wish to acknowledge and give special thanks to Dr. James Scott and Dr. Kelly Shaw of the European Union Center at the University of Missouri-Columbia for assisting and supporting me in the organization of the e-health conference and the invitation of guest speakers from different parts of the world. Furthermore, I would like to thank Dr. Gordon Brown, Chair of the Health Management and Informatics Department and Dr. Joyce Mitchell, Director of Informatics and Director of the National Library of Medicine Biomedical and Health Informatics Training Program at the University of

Missouri-Columbia for their advice and support, and David Moxley, Associate Director of the Executive Informatics Program, for his valuable assistance in the editorial process.

Contents

Message from James K. Scott, Director of the European Union Center at the University of Missouri

James K. SCOTT, PhD
European Union Center
University of Missouri-Columbia
USA

e-Health is usually defined as the use of information technology applications with the aim to support healthcare delivery and education. Beyond the use of new tools and software and hardware applications, e-health refers to a fundamental redesign of healthcare delivery.

e-Health in the European Union (EU) has great potential to improve efficiency when patients cross national boundaries to seek treatment in other EU member states and to enable medical facilities and services within the EU to be linked and accessible to all EU citizens.

Here, in the United States, key policy-makers, researchers and practitioners recognize the value of information technology in addressing our nation's healthcare challenges. According to a recent Institute of Medicine report, "to deliver healthcare in the 21st century, the system must have a health information and communications technology infrastructure that is accessible to all patients and providers." In his recent State of the Union, President Bush proposed to double the budget to $100 million for demonstration projects related to health information technology, which will save lives and help to reduce costs. President Bush emphasized the importance of electronic medical records and advanced information technologies in health care.

It is clear that technological advances will revolutionize the health care field. The key challenge for informatics professionals is to design and implement applications and systems that are driven not by technology features, but by users' needs. Towards this end, the European Union Center at the University of Missouri sponsored a conference entitled "e-health: Current Status and Future Trends in the EU and the US" in February, 2004. This conference was designed to facilitate dialogue between researchers, policy makers and health care providers of both continents. It addressed a broad range of issues such as mobile technologies in health care, "smart home" technologies, bioinformatics, telemedicine applications, Internet applications in health care, legislative efforts, ethical and security concerns associated with the diffusion of e-health. The book chapters that follow, represent a distillation of the rich, practical discussion that ensued.

E-Health: Current Status and Future Trends
G. Demiris (Ed.)
IOS Press, 2004

A Comprehensive Model for Evaluating Telemedicine

Lanis L. HICKS, Ph.D.
Keith E. BOLES, Ph.D.
Department of Health Management and Informatics
School of Medicine
University of Missouri-Columbia
USA

Abstract. Increasingly, telecommunications and advanced information technologies are being used for a variety of activities: clinical, administrative, and education/research. These activities are undertaken with the expectation that health care delivery will be improved. To validate this expectation, a number of investigations have been undertaken to assess the effectiveness and efficiency of the activities. Unfortunately, many of these investigations have either been incomplete or have applied inappropriate techniques in the evaluation process. This is especially true in the attempts to evaluate the cost effectiveness of various telecommunication technologies and service delivery. The model presented here provides a systematic framework that can be used in evaluating the effectiveness, efficiency, and feasibility of telemedicine. The model delineates the different aspects and characteristics of an evaluation across three dimensions—focus (cost, quality, access), level (individual, community, society), and activities (clinical, administration, education/research). These dimensions are interrelated, making comprehensive evaluation difficult.

The health care industry is changing rapidly, especially with the introduction of new technologies and organizational structures. A technology that has the potential for significantly shaping future transactions and relationships in the health care arena is telemedicine. Telemedicine has evolved tremendously from its initial debut in the 1960s with the provision of medical consultations and treatments via the telephone by remote providers. While the distance concept is still present, the technologies involved have changed dramatically. Broadly defined, however, telemedicine is still "the use of electronic information and communications technologies to provide and support health care when distance separates the participants."[1] Telemedicine has the potential to make positive contributions to improvements in the performance of the health care system by increasing access to quality services, transferring expert knowledge, and reducing geographic barriers. However, for its potential to be realized, its value must be convincingly demonstrated.

In discussing telemedicine, it is important to keep in mind that telemedicine is not a new medical technique. Rather, telemedicine is simply a way of delivering the same health interventions through a different media. Telemedicine simply enables the exchange of information and provision of services across geographic, time, and social boundaries. Telemedicine equipment can, however, be used for multiple purposes; therefore, its value to these multiple users must be evaluated. However, as reported elsewhere, [2], [3], [4], [5] previous evaluations have been incomplete, focusing on limited applications or dimensions, or have used inappropriate techniques in the evaluation process. For telemedicine to achieve its full potential, its value (benefits) must be aggressively evaluated on a comprehensive and appropriate basis.

Concept of Evaluation

Evaluations are undertaken with the intent to determine the impact, or consequences, of an intervention. In general, evaluations are one of two types: prospective or retrospective. Prospective evaluation uses past events and reactions to those events to project what would probably occur if a specific event happened or an intervention was implemented. Retrospective evaluation, on the other hand, assesses what actually changed after an event or intervention occurred. In either case, the intent of the evaluation is to assess the change that occurs when an event or intervention occurs.

In a clinical setting, evaluation attempts to determine what occurs either in the prevention, diagnosis, treatment, or eradication of a particular disease or illness with the application of a particular medication, procedure, device, or behavior modification strategy. Historically, in clinical evaluations, attention focused on the evaluative factors of safety and efficacy. Today, however, it is increasingly important to include economic feasibility and implications in the evaluation of medical technologies and interventions.[6], [7] Economic evaluations add the determination of the resources that would have to be expended to implement the intervention. This emerging additional objective increases the complexity of the evaluation process, increasing the need for a multidisciplinary research team.

Theoretical Foundation

The theoretical foundation for the proposed model is transactional economics, also referred to as transaction cost economics.[8] It is based on the premise that health care services involve complex sequences of exchanges, or transactions, among various stakeholders—patients, providers, payers, regulators, etc.—and that there are costs incurred in the transactions beyond those associated with the labor, supplies, and equipment needed to produce the output. Some of the transactions are concrete and observable (surgery, prescriptions, imaging, laboratory work, etc.), but the majority of the transactions in health care are intangible and abstract (information, consultations, advice, etc.).[9] In the production of health care, numerous stakeholders interact (perform transactions), on a periodic or continuing basis, and these exchanges require the coordination of the details involved in the transaction. As mentioned earlier, transactions in the medical market are complex, and these transactions drive the triad access, quality, and cost associated with the system.

The introduction of telemedicine alters the context of the transactions in the health care system. When the telecommunications structure is superimposed on that of existing transactions in the health care system, then the scope and complexity of the transactions will be modified, magnified, or diminished. With the introduction of telemedicine, the nature of the previous exchanges is changed, and the value of those changes needs to be assessed. The proposed evaluation model is designed to examine the extent to which changes in the transactions impact the interactions among the various stakeholders. The intent is to be able to use the model to determine the added value derived from the use of telemedicine in the delivery and support of health care services.

One important element for assessing the consequences of the introduction of telemedicine is through its impact on transactional distance.[10] Transactional distance refers to any factor having an impact on the interaction that creates distance among the parties involved in the transaction—education, knowledge or information, culture, ethnicity, gender, health status, geography, etc. Geography primarily creates distance through time and space. When parties are geographically dispersed, substantial costs can be associated with traveling to a mutual location where the transaction can occur. In addition, telemedicine offers the advantage of not necessarily requiring all participants in an encounter to be at the same place at the same time for the transaction to occur. Telemedicine attempts to enhance the value of the transaction by reducing the transactional distance and its associated costs.

Three-Dimensional Model

The comprehensive evaluation model presented here is intended to provide a systematic framework that encompasses the totality of factors and issues to be included in the assessment of telemedicine. As depicted graphically in Figure 1, the three dimensions of evaluation consist of:

1. Level of analysis—individual, community, society
2. Focus of analysis—cost, quality, access
3. Activities of analysis—clinical, education/research, administration

The top of the cube represents a variety of stakeholders, or the level of analysis. The front of the cube represents the driving forces of health care, or the focus of analysis. The end of the cube represents the different uses of telemedicine, or the activities of analysis.

Figure 1: Comprehensive Model

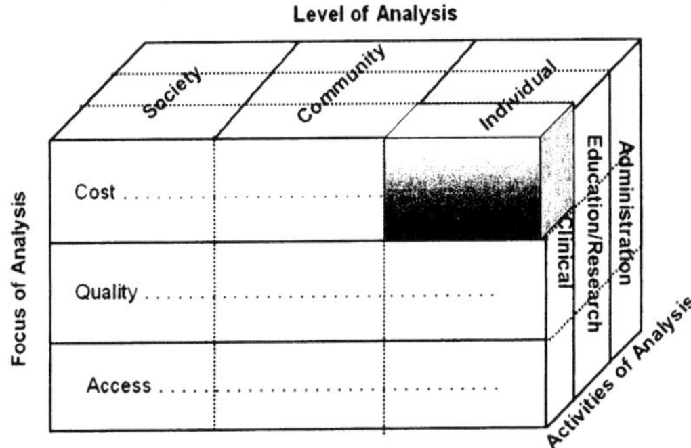

This three-dimensional approach to the evaluation of telemedicine forces consideration of the myriad of issues involved in the delivery of services through this media. Any evaluation undertaken should make explicit the dimensions included in the analysis. For example, as illustrated in the highlighted cell in Figure 1, the level of analysis in this partial evaluation is the individual, the focus of analysis is cost, and the activity of analysis is clinical. In a comprehensive evaluation, all elements of all three dimensions would need to be included.

Level of Analysis

The first dimension considered is the level of analysis. There are three broad categories involved in the level of analysis—individual, community, and society. Each of these three broad categories can be subdivided into multiple elements. It is critical to identify the level at which the analysis takes place in order to ensure that the appropriate benefits and costs are being captured. Conclusions regarding the acceptability of telemedicine may vary substantially across the three levels, since benefits and costs may accrue to entities outside the immediate transaction.

Individual Level

At the individual level, concern is focused on the direct benefits and costs associated with the individual and his/her problem. At this level, concerns will tend to be narrower than at the other levels, since the tendency is to focus on "what will it cost me, and how will I benefit (gain) from the exchange." At the individual level, it is also very important to identify the specific perspective of the individual element considered, since this will impact the values included in the benefits and costs. The individual level can be further divided into more specific elements—patient, caregiver, provider (physician, nurse, therapist, technician, etc.), payer (public or private), technology suppliers, etc. For example, if the focus of the evaluation at the individual level is the patient, then the benefits/costs captured in the assessment may be very different than if the focus was the payer for the service.

Community Level

The second level of analysis is the community. A community is loosely defined as a group of people who occupy an analogous location in social, economic, or institutional structures. A community is not simply limited to geographical boundaries, but rather it is comprised of a complex network, intertwining the political, social, and economic relationships within a group of people. These groups, by definition, pursue common interests and objectives, often exchanging ideas, goods, and services in an effort to obtain those goals. These goals strive to better the well-being of the community, as a whole, and not simply certain individuals within a community. A community consists of a common bond—a web connecting all members and components of the community to each other.[11] Thus, a community is more than the sum of its parts.

As each individual piece is placed in the community puzzle, a new whole is created. This new whole is able to overcome former obstacles blocking individuals. As a result, community issues may not directly reflect individual interest; however, such issues will directly affect each individual within the community. For economic analysis, the economic impact on a community is generally much greater than the sum of the impacts on the individuals within the community.

Due to the close-knit, interconnected nature of a community, the general health of its members has a major effect on the well-being of the community's social and financial institutions. For example, the production function of a community is impacted by the extent to which its members are able and willing to purchase health care and other major lifestyle commodities in the local market. This phenomenon makes it exceedingly difficult for the community to measure accurately the benefits and costs associated with medical interventions.

For the evaluation of telemedicine, the community can be further subdivided into at least two elements—the hub community and the distant, or remote, community. The specific community considered in the evaluation will have an impact on the costs and benefits included in the analysis. In evaluating telemedicine, it is also important to consider the interrelationships between the two communities. For example, while keeping patients in a local community for services through the provision of care via telemedicine will also keep the resources of the patients in that local community, it will decrease the resources available in the hub community because the patient (and possibly the patient's family and friends) won't travel to the hub community and make additional purchases while there. These interactions and focus need to be explicitly stated in the evaluation study.

Societal Level

The third level of analysis is that of society. A society is a relatively autonomous population whose members share a cultural identity and way of life, interact in patterned ways, and reside in a common geographic territory.[12] This perspective is the broadest, encompassing such factors as income and health distributions of the population. Once again, the whole is not merely the sum of its parts. Societal benefits and costs extend beyond both the individuals within a community and the communities themselves. For example, a social benefit is enjoyed when all individuals in society are inoculated against infectious diseases. Individuals remain healthy and communities remain productive because of the inoculations. Likewise, a social cost is incurred when individuals attempt to be a free rider by not receiving an inoculation because of the belief that everyone else will receive an inoculation and they, therefore, will not be exposed to sick individuals. Too many individuals thinking in this manner can result in an outbreak, leaving the individuals at even greater risk of exposure. Furthermore, if an outbreak occurs, community production rates fall, as more individuals have to miss work due to illness. This illustration serves to exemplify further the influence of societal factors on both individuals and communities.

A key distinction between community and society is that society includes numerous communities. Thus, as interactions take place between and among communities, society can either gain or lose. If one community is able to improve its health status, or reduce the crime rate, etc., then other communities are impacted. An infected individual from one community may transmit a disease or infection to another community. Production facilities may decide to locate in one community as opposed to another, due to the technological innovations available. Whereas externalities (social benefits and/or costs) exist at both the individual and community levels, there can be no externalities where society is concerned.

The society level can also be subdivided into smaller elements, especially with the implementation of telemedicine. A society can be considered internal to a country or it can be considered global, encompassing members of more than one country. As geographic distances are bridged through telemedicine use, the political boundaries of countries are also bridged. Figure 2 provides a more detailed illustration of the different elements in the three levels of analysis. As depicted in this graph, numerous "cells" are added to the three-dimensional model, as greater detail is considered in the evaluation.

Figure 2: Detailed Level of Analysis

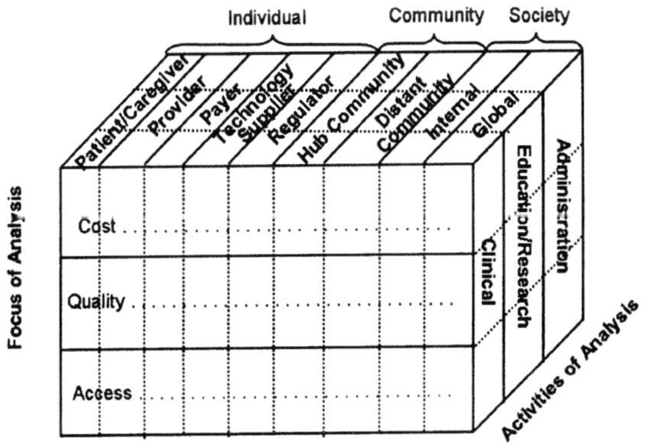

Focus of Analysis

The second dimension considered is the focus of the analysis. In recent years, much attention has focused on balancing the triad cost, quality, and access in health care. Each of these elements is important in its own right, and each plays a pivotal role in the political and economic discussions regarding the future of health care. Each is also critically important as new technologies are introduced and reforms occur.

Cost

Typically, when the cost of health care is discussed, the reference is to the expenditures made for health care. These expenditures have been increasing rapidly in recent years. In 2003, it is estimated that health care expenditures in the United States reached $1.67 trillion, accounting for 15.3 percent of the Gross Domestic Product (GDP). While the rate of increase slowed in 2003, it is predicted that the expenditures on health care will outpace economic growth in the United States during the next decade. As a result, it is predicted that expenditures will be $3.36 trillion in 2013, accounting for 18.4 percent of the GDP.[13] The magnitude of expenditures in this sector, and the increase it accounts for in the GDP, will continue to focus attention on controlling the costs of health care in the future.

While there is no evidence that the United States is necessarily spending too much on health care, there is a growing concern that sufficient value is not being achieved with the dollars spent on this sector. As health care consumes a larger and larger share of the GDP, concerns are growing around what is being sacrificed to accomplish this. While there is no consensus among the population about the amount that should be spent on health care,[14] pressure is growing for decision-makers to demonstrate the value of investments made. This position reflects the societal dimension discussed in the level of analysis section. If investments in and utilization of telemedicine is to be sustainable, it must be demonstrated to be cost effective, at least at some level of analysis.

In assessing costs, the basic economic concept of marginalism is applied: compared with the traditional method, what is the incremental change in cost associated with the use of telemedicine? While an increase in cost is not necessarily inappropriate, the value gained with the increase would need to be shown also. In determining the costs of telemedicine, both direct and indirect costs must be included. The direct costs reflect such things as the equipment, connection and transmission costs, staff time, professional services, supplies, etc. Indirect costs reflect such items as other medical services used as a result of the telemedicine encounter, a change in the type of services used because of access, additional social services used, etc. Many times, the indirect costs are larger than the direct costs (but indirect benefits/gains are also often greater than direct benefits). The key is to capture all relevant impacts of the intervention.

Health care has an important role in the economy, serving multiple functions. Not only are health care providers the source of medical care, but they also serve as key employers, substantial supporters of local business, and magnets for social agencies and other medical services.[15], [16] Telemedicine can reduce costs by saving patients money and time by being able to receive services locally. Further evaluation of cost-reducing implications of telemedicine is needed.

Cost is also important at the community and individual levels. Daily newspapers abound regarding the cost of this procedure or that, and of the increasing impact of prescription drugs on health care costs.[17] At the local level, hospitals complain that cost containment efforts are making it impossible to keep their doors open, especially those located in rural regions of the country.[18] Physicians bristle at the idea that cost should be considered when making medical decisions, while payers insist that this be done.[19] Regardless of the social issues involving the extent to which economics should play a role in medical decision making, it is obvious that costs will play a role in the future development of health care.[20]

Quality

The quality issue is receiving tremendous attention currently. Outcomes research and evidence-based medicine are widespread in today's environment.[21] If telemedicine is to be widely accepted, then the quality of care provided through this mechanism must be established. In establishing the quality of services, it is important to evaluate not only the clinical quality of the encounter, but also the patient and provider satisfaction and acceptance. In terms of the technology, assuming no malfunctions, quality is based on a comparison of the visual and audio interactions provided by telemedicine with those of a physical face-to-face encounter.[22],[23]

There are still some risk and uncertainty involved with the use of new technologies that do not have 100 percent reliability. As long as there is the possibility of data and information interruption, thereby interfering with the interaction, acceptance of the technology will be delayed. Similar interference takes place, however, as long as flat tires, mechanical problems, and weather-related travel interruptions work to prevent a patient's clinic visit.

Likewise, even with telemedicine and telecommunications technology, the issue of performance, or quality measurement, plays a major role. The interaction through the technology creates some anxiety on the part of both parties to the encounter regarding the ability to ensure the quality of the interaction. In some cases, it may be necessary to provide clinical trials in order to ensure that quality is not compromised. Once again, quality measures, the use of clinical trials, and evidence-based medicine, are all relatively recent phenomena. The increase in transactional distance through the introduction of telemedicine adds only one more layer of complexity to the equation, making evaluation more difficult.

As the public receives more information from the reporting of hospital, physician, and health plan utilization and outcomes, quality will play an increasingly important role in health decision making.[24] Employees will demand that their employers contract with high quality providers. Employers and health plans will make increasing use of centers of excellence, as research indicates long-term costs are reduced, by channeling services to high volume providers.[25] The quality issue is very closely related to cost, encouraging the use of benefit-cost or cost-effectiveness analyses.

Access

Telemedicine has the ability to improve access to medical services in areas where specialists and technologies are not available. Access can be improved with telemedicine by making another technology or specialist available, or by supplementing the existing array of services available locally.

While much of the access debate has revolved around the uninsured and underinsured at the national level, this is also a major issue at the local level. Rural hospitals are experiencing declining occupancy and reduced reimbursement for those patients being served.[26] Individuals residing in rural areas may or may not have access to a readily accessible hospital or emergency room, or even a primary care physician.[27] To the extent that society wishes to support a lifestyle, or reduce urban population, activities to encourage or support rural lifestyle should be considered. This is a social issue, which should be addressed explicitly. Telemedicine has the ability to provide some of the advantages of an urban community, such as access to specialist physicians and educational opportunities, while preserving some of the advantages of rural living, such as lower population density, and rural activities such as farming or other agricultural activities.

In summary, any changes to the system, any innovations, any clinical developments, any new drugs, must all be evaluated in terms of their impact on these three areas: cost, quality, and access. Increasing health care costs, both in real terms, and as a proportion of the national budget, has resulted in a major push to reduce health care costs.[28], [29] Likewise, there is an increasing emphasis being placed on the efficacy of medical treatments and the quality of services provided.[30] This has led to increasing reliance being placed on the outcomes and quality implications of health-related activities. Finally, the last area to be considered is access.[31] Access to health services is still important, related to both uninsured and underinsured, and access to health services is also important to individuals residing in remote and isolated areas of the country–including most rural and inner-city areas.

The cost, quality, and access foci are important to the three levels of analysis: individual, community, and societal. Any evaluation must be explicit about the specific level being addressed.

Activities of Analysis

The third dimension of any evaluation study is an exploration of the activities supported by the telecommunication resources. Once the technology and equipment are in place, telecommunication can take place for a variety of reasons. The most common (and possibly the most valued) use of telemedicine resources are for clinical examinations, consultations, discussions, and other clinical purposes involving improvement in the diagnosis, treatment, and other decision making relative to a specific patient.[32] This, however, is not the only use for the equipment, and indeed, with a little creativity, the technology can be used for a variety of functions.

Clinical

Telemedicine technology, at least in its present form, has been used more often in some specialties than others. The broadest uses of the video and audio telemedicine interactions so far are in the areas of radiology, psychiatry, and dermatology, with cardiology and other areas following.[33], [34], [35], [36] Psychiatry has been found to be a viable use, due to the interpersonal relationships involved, without the need for a physical examination to take place. On the other hand, dermatological cameras, under the hand of a skillful assistant, have been found to provide sufficient resolution on the receiving end for the physician to make confident diagnoses.[37] Experience at the University of Missouri has also found acceptance among cardiologists for the use of telemedicine for follow-up visits. The numbers of follow-up visits have been increasing, improving patient compliance, and both patient and physician comfort with the encounter.

There is a great deal of flexibility in the use of telemedicine resources, where tactile examination is not needed. Otoscopes, stethoscopes, and other examination equipment have been specially designed for use with telemedicine equipment, and have been found to be at least as good as, and in come cases better than, those used in face-to-face encounters. For instance, otoscope views can be examined on a 27-inch TV monitor, providing a much better view, with excellent resolution.[38]

As the technology improves, there will be a broadening of the potential clinical applications of telemedicine. There are already experimental demonstrations of the performance of surgery over a distance.[39] Likewise, virtual reality holds the potential for three-dimensional examination, along with tactile and even internal examinations to be performed.[40]

Education/Research

There are other, non-clinical, uses of the resources that also enhance its value. For instance, the same telecommunications resources used for clinical encounters can be used for training professionals and other (provider and patient) educational purposes. Educational uses of the equipment can enhance its value, and have some of the same benefits in terms of reduced travel time and other value to the community.

There are a variety of education functions that can be enhanced. Continuing medical education (CME) credits can be provided to a widely distributed audience from a central site. Resident training can be provided from a teaching facility to residents located in rural areas. Telecommunications equipment can be placed on rolling tables, allowing for exceptional mobility. The technology is easily connected to large screens, making it easily accessible to large groups of individuals. This permits the use of the technology to reach larger bodies, and is especially amenable to a classroom setting. The content can then be in the form of didactic materials, or actual case studies, or even for transmission of an actual patient encounter (with appropriate permission and approval, of course). The important point here is that there is a great deal of flexibility–in terms of where the technology can be used, the number of individuals involved, and the form of the education taking place.

Telemedicine also has the potential to be used in research. When large patient bases are required for the study, it may be possible to enroll patients at distant sites without requiring extensive travel. Similarly, surveys and other research activities can be conducted using this technology.

Administrative

The third use of the telemedicine equipment is for the performance of administrative functions. Virtual meetings can be held among geographically dispersed individuals, enhancing the timeliness of and attendance at such meetings, and reducing the amount of time and money spent on travel. This is particularly true in today's environment of multi-organizational systems, and the expanding network requirements of managed care. Dispersed participants can meet more often, share more democratically in the decision making, and therefore, bring value to the organization through greater input.

For example, meetings can be set up between two individuals, or among large groups of individuals. The number of individuals involved at any one site is constrained only by the size of the room. The same equipment used for teaching can be used for meetings. For instance, most telemedicine setups include an easy mechanism to transmit slides or transparencies, or even the printed page. This function is valuable, whether the application is clinical, educational, or administrative. Portability of the telemedicine equipment will only be enhanced in the future, making it easier to shift from clinical to education to administrative use of the equipment. Price will also be reduced, making it easier to have more than one set of equipment.

Conclusions

The model presented here provides a comprehensive overview of the elements to be considered in the evaluation of telemedicine. Previous studies have dealt with different levels, foci, and activities of this technology. Most are specific to clinical uses, usually a specific clinical specialty, or even procedure, and have been limited either to quality, cost, or access issues. While not inappropriate, such studies fail to capture the total implications of telemedicine. Future studies should incorporate more comprehensive elements, or at least explicitly indicate the level, focus, and activities of analysis included. In a comprehensive evaluation, all elements of all three dimensions would need to be included.

References

[1] Committee on Evaluating Clinical Applications of Telemedicine (1996). Telemedicine: A Guide to Assessing Telecommunications in Health Care (MJ Field, ed). Washington DC: National Academy Press. p.1.
[2] Adams ME, NT McCall, et. al. (1992). "Economic Analysis in Randomized Control Trials." Medical Care 30(3): 231-243.
[3] Argo KE, CA Bradley, et. al. (1997). "Sensitivity Analysis in Health Economic and Pharmacoeconomic Studies: An Appraisal of the Literature." Pharmacoeconomics 11(1): 75-88.
[4] Birch S, and A Gafni. (1992). "Cost-Effectiveness/Utility Analyses: Do Current Decision Rules Lead Us to Where We Want to Be?" Journal of Health Economics 11(3): 279-296.
[5] Blumenschein K and M Johannesson. (1996). "Economic Evaluation in Healthcare. A Brief History and Future Directions." Pharmacoeconomics 10(2): 114-122.
[6] Boyer JG and DS Pathak. (1994). "Establishing Value through Pharmacoeconomics: The Emerging Third Objective in Clinical Trials." Topics in Hospital Pharmacy Management 13(4): 1-10.
[7] Chalfin DB. (1998). "Evidence-Based Medicine and Cost-Effectiveness Analysis." Critical Care Clinics 14(3): 525-537.
[8] Milgrom P and J Roberts. (1992). Economics, Organization and Management. Englewood Cliffs NJ: Prentice Hall.
[9] Stiles RA, Mick SS, Wise CG. (2001). "The Logic of Transaction Cost Economics in Health Care Organization Theory." Health Care Management Review 26(2): 85-92.
[10] Milgrom P and J Roberts. (1992).
[11] Kindig DA. (1997). Purchasing Population Health: Paying for Results. Ann Arbor MI: University of Michigan Press.
[12] Ibid.
[13] Heffler S, S Smith, et. al. (2004). "Health Spending Projections through 2013." Health Affairs (Web Exclusive) @4-79.
[14] Eddy DM. (1990). "Connecting Value and Costs: Whom Do We Ask, and What Do We Ask Them?" Journal of the American Medical Association 264(13): 1737-1739.
[15] Hart LG, BA Amundson, RA Rosenblatt (1990). "Is There a Role for the Small Rural Hospital?" Journal of Rural Health 6(2).
[16] Shreffler MJ (1996). "An Ecological View of the Rural Environment: Levels of Influence on Access to Health Care." Advanced Nursing Science 18(4): 48-59.
[17] Etheredge L (1999). "Purchasing Medicare Prescription Drug Benefits: A New Proposal." Health Affairs 18(4): 7-19.
[18] Langland-Orban B, LC Gapenski, WB Vogel (1996). "Differences in Characteristics of Hospitals with Sustained High and Sustained Low Profitability." Hospital and Health Services Administration 41(3): 385-399.
[19] Jacobson PD (1999). "Legal Challenges to Managed Care Cost Containment Programs: An Initial Assessment." Health Affairs 18(4): 69-85.

[20] Heffler S, M. Freeland (1999). "The Next Decade of Health Spending: A New Outlook." Health Affairs 18(4): 86-95.
[21] Balas EA, S Austin Boren; LL Hicks et. al. (1998). "Effects of Linking Practice Data to Published Evidence: A Randomized Controlled Trial of Clinical Direct Reports." Medical Care 36: 79-82.
[22] Phillips CM, WA Burke, A Shechter, et. al. (1997). "Reliability of Dermatology Teleconsultantations with the Use of Teleconferencing Technology." Journal of American Academy of Dermatology 37(3): 398-402.
[23] Finley JP, GP Sharratt, MA Nanton et. al. (1997). "Paediatric Echocardiology by Telemedicine: Nine Years' Experience." Journal of Telemedicine and Telecare 3(11): 200-204.
[24] Chen J, MJ Radford, Y Wang, et al (1999). "Performance of the '100 Top Hospitals': What Does the Report Card Report." Health Affairs 18(4): 53-68.
[25] Rees T (1997). "Top Hospital Designation Rates Ad Series: South Carolina University Medical Center Highlights Its Centers of Excellence." Profiles in Healthcare Marketing 13(6): 29-32.
[26] Schoeman JA (1999). "Impact of the BBA on Medicare HMO Payments for Rural Areas." Health Affairs 18(1): 244-254.
[27] Politzer RM, SR Gamliel, JM Cultice, et al (1996). "Matching Physician Supply and Requirements: Testing Policy Recommendations." Inquiry 33(2): 181-194.
[28] Iglehart JK (1999). "The American Health Care System: Expenditures." New England Journal of Medicine 340(1): 70-76.
[29] Smith S, M Freeland, S Heffler, D McKusick (1998).
[30] Bodenheimer T (1999). "The American Health Care System: The Movement for Improved Quality in Health Care." New England Journal of Medicine 340(6): 488-492.
[31] Kuttner R (1999). "The American Health Care System: Health Insurance Coverage." New England Journal of Medicine 340(2): 163-168.
[32] Field MJ editor (1996). Telemedicine: A Guide to Assessing Telecommunications in Health Care Washington DC: National Academy Press.
[33] Franken EA (1996). "Teleradiology: Moving into the Mainstream." Telemedicine Today 4(1): 25-28.
[34] Allen A, D Allen (1994). "Telemental Health Services Today." Telemedicine Today 2(1): 12-24.
[35] Burgess SG, CE Julius, HW Watson et al (1997). "Telemedicine for Dermatology Care in Rural Patients." Telemedicine Journal 3(3): 215-225.
[36] Hassol A, C Irvin, G Gaumer et al (1997). "Rural Applications of Telemedicine." Telemedicine Journal 3(3): 215-225.
[37] Federman D, D Hogan, JR Taylor (1995). "A Comparison of Diagnosis, Evaluation, and Treatment of patients with Dermatologic Disorders." Journal of the American Academy of Dermatology 32: 726-729
[38] Norton SA, AE Burdic, CM Phillips, B Berman (1997). "Teledermatology and Underserved Populations." Archives of Dermatology 133: 197-200.
[39] Eadie LH, AM Seifalian, and BR Davidson. (2003). "Telemedicine in Surgery." British Journal of Surgery 90: 647-658.
[40] National Library of Medicine Project. Organ Modeling in Support of Virtual Surgery Simulation.

E-Health: Current Status and Future Trends
G. Demiris (Ed.)
IOS Press, 2004

Home Based E-Health Applications

George DEMIRIS, PhD
Department of Health Management and Informatics
School of Medicine, University of Missouri-Columbia, USA

Abstract. Home based e-health applications use telecommunication and video-conferencing technologies to enable a healthcare provider at the clinical site to communicate with patients at their home. Such an interaction is called a 'virtual visit'. Numerous applications are utilizing commercially available monitoring devices and the Internet to enable home based disease management and monitoring. The aim to meet older adults' desire to remain independent at home while controlling home health care costs has also led to the development of "smart home" technologies. A smart home is a residence equipped with technology that enhances safety of patients at home and monitors their health conditions. Therefore, the devices and sensors chosen to be installed and maintained in the older adults' residences need to address functional limitations and social and health care needs. This paper provides an overview of home based e-health applications and discusses the challenges of implementing and evaluating e-health applications.

1. Introduction

Home health care is a growing component of the current health system that refers to care services that are provided to individuals, their family members and caregivers in their home or other home-like settings. These services can be short or long-term and include nursing, rehabilitation, social work and home health assistance. More than 20,000 providers deliver home care services to approximately eight million individuals diagnosed with acute illness, long-term health conditions, permanent disability, or terminal illness [1]. Increased life-expectancy, population growth and funding limitations could threaten the viability of home health care. In the year 2030 citizens over the age of 65 years are projected to represent 20% of the US population [2]. Thus, Medicare and Social Security programs are facing financial challenges as the ratio of workers paying taxes to retirees drawing benefits has long been decreasing.

The rapid growth of the elderly population and increase in life expectancy have led to new models of positive ageing where older adults are being empowered to lead fulfilling lives and adapt to degenerative changes to maintain functionality, autonomy and quality of life. Independence is a critical issue for many older adults as they age. However, in the pursuit of independence, often the older adult's safety and health are at risk as they try to cope with health-related issues such as falls, sensory impairment, immobility, isolation, and medication non-compliance.

Home based e health applications are viewed as a method of healthcare delivery that could address issues of cost and limitations of access to homecare, both for rural and urban underserved patients. In this paper, we will provide an overview of home based e-health applications and discuss the concept of telehomecare and that of smart homes. The first demonstrates how technology can enhance current home care services, whereas the concept of smart homes refers to an emerging trend of non-obtrusive disease prevention and monitoring of residents who are not necessarily home care patients.

2. The concept of telehomecare

One area of home based e-health applications is telehomecare, or telemedicine in home care, based on the utilization of telecommunication and videoconferencing technologies to enable a healthcare provider at the clinical site to communicate with patients at their home. Such an interaction via videoconferencing is called a 'virtual visit'. In this context, the term 'actual visit' is used to describe the traditional visit of the healthcare provider to the patient's home that includes a "face-to-face" interaction.

The advancements in portable monitoring technologies and the diffusion of the Internet led to an increase of the number of telehomecare applications in the 1990s. The use of trans-telephonic exercise monitoring as an alternative for cardiac rehabilitation patients unable to return to a hospital-based program was introduced and evaluated in 1993 [3]. The evaluation was carried out within a randomized controlled trial and the findings suggest that this type of monitoring can be an effective supplement to hospital-based monitoring. Another application of the early 90s was a telemedicine system for self-monitoring and dietetic education of diabetic patients [4]. The system was found to have a positive impact on patients' dietetic knowledge and several clinical outcomes (total cholesterol, LDL-cholesterol). A randomized controlled trial in 1996 by Friedman et al [5] demonstrated a positive effect of automated telephone patient monitoring and counseling on patient adherence to anti-hypertensive medications and on blood pressure control. Johnston et al [6] evaluated the use and costs of remote video technology in the home care setting and determined that this approach achieved cost savings and improved access to home care support while producing no differences in clinical outcomes when compared to traditional home care.

The World Wide Web has been proven as an important tool for numerous home based disease management applications. Such applications have been developed for a wide range of clinical applications such as monitoring of asthma (e.g. the home asthma telemonitoring (HAT) [7] system which assists patients in the daily routine of asthma care with personalized interventions), diabetes (e.g. the Diabetes Care Management Support System (DCMSS) to support care delivery to diabetic patients [8] or the Telematic Management of Insulin-Dependent Diabetes Mellitus (T-IDDM) project funded by the European Union [9]) and post transplant care. The TeleHomeCare Project at the University of Minnesota also utilized the Internet aiming to enable patients at home diagnosed with congestive heart failure, chronic obstructive pulmonary disease or requiring wound care to interact with health care providers at the agency. Personalized web pages allowed patients to interact with their providers and fill out daily questionnaires including questions about vital signs (such as weight, blood pressure or temperature), symptoms, and overall well-being and nutrition. Alerts were triggered and providers were notified when a patient's entry required immediate medical attention based on predefined personalized rules [10].

While there is a plethora of telehomecare interventions and products, we are still lacking evidence of its effectiveness that would result from randomized clinical trials. We searched (in February 2004) the following electronic databases: Medline, Science Citation Index, Social Sciences Citation Index, Arts and Humanities Citation Index and the TIE (Telemedicine Information Exchange) database. Searches were restricted to English language papers and the keywords used were: "telemedicine," "home based," "home care," telehomecare," "home telecare." The papers identified were then hand searched for other relevant references. We included only studies that used quantitative and/or qualitative methods to explore the value of telehomecare applications; thus, review or discussion papers were excluded. A total of 17 studies were identified. Of these studies, seven [6,11-16] followed the design of a randomized controlled trial. Two of these studies are especially noteworthy, due to the statistically significant results: the study by Jerant et al [11] found that mean CHF related readmission charges were 86% lower in the experimental (telehomecare) group than in the group receiving traditional care; the study by Johnston et al [6] found no difference in quality indicators and patient satisfaction between the experimental and control group; however, a significant decrease of total mean costs of care was realized for the experimental group. A multi-state cost analysis study determined that the average cost of a telemedicine visit was only around one-fifth the cost of a traditional nursing visit [17].

In most of these studies, several commercially available portable medical devices were used for client monitoring, including portable spirometers and pulse oximeters [13], portable ECG and blood pressure devices [18], and innovative devices for specific target groups [19,20]. These devices are tested for accuracy and are approved by FDA before they become available on the market. In some cases, data are stored in the device and retrieved at a later point or are displayed on a monitor at completion of the test session. Devices that allow the automatic transmission of data over regular phone lines or in accordance with the system's transmission architecture are preferred over devices where the patient has to read the results and announce them to a nurse during a virtual visit. The latter can impose a burden to elderly or visually impaired patients and impact the test accuracy.

In addition to monitoring devices, videoconferencing products are used in telehomecare to enable the interaction of patients at home with health care providers at the remote site. Videoconferencing at the patients' homes without the cost of upgrading the existing infrastructure has been enabled by the International Telecommunication Union--Telecommunication Sector (ITU-T) standard H.324 for multimedia conferencing on plain-old telephone service (POTS). H.324 defines standards for transmitting video, audio, and other data over one analog telephone line. As local and wide area networks use same interoperable substandards as H.324, a great extent of interoperability among videophones with different features and by different manufacturers can be achieved. Videophones can be installed into the patients' home and operated over the regular phone lines. Training required for patients is in many cases minimal, as videophones operate like regular phones with the addition of a screen. If a low-cost approach is not a priority, there is the option to utilize an advanced infrastructure if one exists or upgrade the existing one to achieve maximum video and audio quality (e.g., by installing ISDN, DSL or T1 lines).

A further, more advanced concept of monitoring is that of wearable sensors. This concept is based on the incorporation of sensors into watches, items of clothing, and eyeglasses. Thus, one could argue that wearable sensors can function as non-invasive in vitro diagnostics tools as they are capable of analyzing, among others, human sweat, tears, stress, strain, and pH increases. One example of wearable sensors is the so called "intelligent knee sleeve" that monitors knee strain or injury [21]. Originally designed for football players, this device is strapped to the knees, and its sleeve provides feedback to users by emitting an audio tone. It can be a useful application for home care patients with mobility impairments or at the rehabilitation phase. Another wearable sensor is a test device for cystic fibrosis [22]. A small portable detector in form of a wristwatch provides test results in minutes, rather than the 24 hours which is the typical response time for a laboratory test. Other devices in form of wrist watches include glucose meters that measure glucose in the interstitial fluid as a low electric current pulls glucose through the skin [23] and a blood oxygen monitor [24]. Finally, sensors can be integrated in clothing items. The "Smart Shirt" incorporates technology into the design of clothing to monitor the wearer's heart rate, EKG, respiration, temperature and vital functions, alerting the wearer or physician if there is a problem [25]. This intervention was initially funded by the U.S. Navy in October 1996 and the Georgia Tech Research Corporation licensed the technology in 2000 to a private company to manufacture and market the product [25].

3. Smart homes

A "smart home" is a residency setting equipped with a set of advanced electronics and automated devices specifically designed for care delivery, remote monitoring, early detection of problems or emergency cases and maximization of patient safety. The origins of the concept are to be found in the late 1970s and the1980s, when "intelligent buildings" were designed with the aim to improve energy efficiency and ventilation. Smart home features usually include motion-sensing devices for automatic lighting control, motorized locks, door and window openers, mobilized blinds and curtains [26], smoke and gas detectors and temperature control devices. Such an infrastructure can address the prevalence of neurological and/or cognitive disorders in the elderly, and enhance their ability to function independently within their residence. The Swedish Handicap Institute operates a demonstration apartment within the SmartBo project [26]. This project focuses on solutions for visually, hearing and mobility impaired residents or residents with cognitive disabilities. It is based on the integration of visual and tactile signaling devices, a text-enlargement program, speech synthesizer, and a Braille display for visually impaired residents within the home. Another smart home demonstration project is PROSAFE, which utilizes a set of infrared motion sensors connected to either a wireless or wired network to support automatic recognition of resident activity, possible falls, and release of alarms, designed specifically for patients with Alzheimers disease [27, 28]. Finally, the Aware Home Research Initiative (AHRI) at Georgia Tech aims to address smart home design challenges and implement interventions that will enhance the quality of life of senior citizens and help them maintain independence while staying at home [29].

Aldrich [30] proposes five hierarchical classes of smart homes:

1) Homes which contain intelligent stand-alone objects
2) Homes which contain intelligent, communicating objects (that exchange information between one another to increase functionality)
3) Connected homes (residencies that have internal and external networks, allowing interactive and remote control of systems, as well as access to services and information, both from within and beyond the home)
4) Learning homes (data are being collected to anticipate users' needs and to adjust the technology's performance accordingly.)
5) Attentive homes (the activity and location of people and objects within the homes are constantly registered in order to control technology in anticipation of the residents' needs.)

This hierarchy sheds light on different levels of communication and data exchange within and beyond the residency. This classification also points out that the extent of discretion given to residents to modify system operational parameters, or the degree of residents' control over system operation can vary. The concept of smart homes is a relatively new one and in spite of numerous pilot projects that demonstrate the technological advances and possible implementation areas, we are still lacking a comprehensive evaluation framework that will address issues such as clinical outcomes and quality of life as well as ethical concerns and challenges.

4. Critical issues for home based e-health applications

Several issues will play a critical role in determining the success and diffusion of home based e-health applications. In the following, we will discuss some of these challenges in the context of e-health.

A great number of patients enrolled in home care or disease management programs are senior citizens and often have functional limitations due to aging and/or their clinical diagnosis. A functional limitation describes a "reduced sensory, cognitive or motor capability associated with human aging, temporary injury, or permanent disability that prevents a person from communicating, working, playing or simply functioning in an environment where other people in the population can function." [31]. While it is often argued that advanced technologies and the Internet have the potential to empower patients and redesign the process of health care delivery, the fastest growing segment of the US population (i.e., people over the age of 50 years) are at a disadvantage as system designers often fail to consider them as a target user group. Usability and accessibility issues are important quality criteria for all web-based interventions; yet, they are frequently ignored by designers and evaluators [32]. Systems targeting home care patients should have reached a high level of functional accessibility [33] and undergone rigorous usability tests. Several design considerations can be taken into account when developing systems for the elderly or other populations with functional limitations [33] such as the avoidance of unnecessary sound effects, choice of appropriate font sizes and colors, etc.

The healthcare sector is facing many challenges in regard to the privacy and confidentiality of individual health information. In the United States, in 1998 the Notice of the Proposed Rule from the Department of Health and Human Services concerning Security and Electronic Signature Standards was introduced [34] as part of the Health Insurance Portability and Accountability Act (HIPAA) that was passed in 1996. This Proposed Rule became law in 2000 in the United States and proposes standards for the security of individual health information and electronic signature use for health care providers, systems and agencies. These standards refer to the security of all electronic health information and have a great impact on the design and operation of electronic applications in home care.

Data transmission over a variety of communication lines such as regular phone lines, satellite or other channels, is often associated with concerns of possible privacy violations. The presence of technical support staff assisting with the transmission procedure at the clinical site could also be perceived as a loss of privacy by the patients. Patients often are unfamiliar with the technical infrastructure and operation of the equipment which can lead to misperceptions of the possibilities of privacy violation during a videoconferencing session. In the context of web based disease management, access to and ownership of the data become critical issues. For many home care applications that use the Internet, patients record monitoring data (such as vital sign and questionnaires) and transmit them daily to a web server owned and maintained by a home care agency or a private third party that allows providers to log in and access their patients' data. Such an application calls for discussion and definition of the issue of data ownership and patients' access rights to parts or all of their records.

Cost analysis and cost-effectiveness studies will inform decisions about payment and reimbursement issues of home based e-health applications. In the United States the Health Care Financing Administration (HCFA) has initially denied Medicare reimbursement of telehomecare on the ground that it has not been proven to be cost-effective. The Balanced Budget Act (BBA) of 1997 has permitted telemedicine reimbursement in specific cases, especially for rural locations that have been classified as healthcare professional shortage areas (HPSA). For those cases reimbursement is provided for Medicare patients staying at home and receiving health care services via telemedicine. In 2000, the Prospective Payment System (PPS went into effect. This system apportions payment per episode of care (using 60 day periods), instead of payment for each visit allowing for home care agencies to integrate virtual visits within the care plan as they see them fit.

The issue of payment and reimbursement is critical for the sustainability of home based e-health applications and does not only refer to reimbursement of virtual visits, but also addresses the financial resources that need to be made available to enable the purchase, installation, and maintenance of the equipment, as well as training of staff and other users.

5. Evaluation of home based e-health applications

An evaluation of home based e-health applications should address both the clinical processes and outcomes, the cost of care and user acceptance.

The measured outcomes of home based e-health applications should be at least the same as of traditional care or they should have a greater positive impact on patients' health. As discussed earlier, this has been investigated to some extent but there is a need for large randomized clinical trials that would demonstrate such an impact. Johnston [6], for example, studied THC's effect on medication compliance and ability for self-care in a quasi-experimental study with a control group (receiving traditional care) and an intervention group (receiving in addition access to a remote video system) and found it to be no different from traditional care. Jerant et al. [11] conducted an one-year randomized trial to assess the effectiveness of home telecare delivered via a 2-way video-conference device with an integrated electronic stethoscope and found that this technology could reduce hospital readmissions and emergency visits for congestive heart failure patients. The premise of most home based e-health applications is that they can enable more intensive and frequent physiological monitoring which can lead to early detection and intervention. They can also support monitoring medication compliance and promoting patient education.

Emphasis should also be placed not only on the clinical outcomes, but the actual processes of care delivery as well. Specifically, it needs to be determined whether video-mediated communication alters the relationship between nurse and patient and decreases quality of care due to the lack of personal contact. Face-to-face interactions are considered "more spontaneous, and free-flowing" than videoconference interactions [35]. It has to further be determined whether the use of videoconferencing technology might intimidate patients and result in their limited participation during the visit. The lack of patient participation is potentially significant because patients tend to value the opportunity to express their concerns, questions and opinions when seeking care [36, 37]. Furthermore, patient participation in medical care often contributes to improved post-consultation outcomes such as greater satisfaction with care [38], greater adherence to treatment recommendations [39], a stronger sense of control [40] and overall more successful disease management [41]. It has yet to be determined whether telemedicine enhances or inhibits patient's communication of their discomfort, symptoms and emotional state, and accordingly, whether it encourages or inhibits doctor's communication of instructions or expressions of empathy [42].

In one study examining the nature of communication in virtual home care visits[10], 122 virtual visits were reviewed and a content analysis was performed to determine themes of interaction. Time was apportioned among the following themes of communication: assessing the patient's clinical status, promoting compliance, addressing psychosocial issues, general informal talk, education, administrative issues, technical issues, assessing patient satisfaction and ensuring accessibility. While there are activities that can clearly not be conducted during a virtual visit, these findings indicate that telehomecare has to potential to address some aspects of an actual visit.

Many home based e-health applications are designed so that the required technology is installed and used in the patient's home and operated by the patients or their surrogate. The success of this form of healthcare delivery obviously requires that patients accept its use. Patients' understanding of the system will influence acceptability and, consequently, the system's rate of diffusion. Thus, it is important to assess patients' perceptions of an e-health system and identify the features they perceive differently after experiencing it. There are not many instruments measuring patients perception of or satisfaction with home based e-health applications that have been tested for reliability and validity. One such instrument is the TMPQ (Telemedicine Perception Questionnaire-copyright University of Minnesota)

[43] which has been developed to assess patients perceptions of the advantages and disadvantages of telehomecare. This instrument was tested extensively and was found to show high level of internal consistency and very high test-retest reliability. The instrument covers domains such as perceived effect on quality of and access to health care, time and money (including time saving for the patient and nurse, and a reduction of costs for the patient and the health care agencies), factors related to the conduct of a virtual visit (including ease of equipment use, equal acceptability of virtual and real visits, protection of privacy and confidentiality, lack of physical contact, reduced sense of intimacy, and the patient's ability to explain medical problems in a virtual visit) and general impression of the concept of telehomecare and its role in the future [43]. Of course, the success of home based e-health applications does not only depend on patients' acceptance, but also on that of the care providers as such systems alter their practice patterns. Nurses and other health care professionals who will be conducting virtual visits, have to accept this mode of communication and be comfortable using the required equipment.

Finally, when assessing the cost of care, one needs to keep in mind that the economic analysis of a home based e-health system is a comparison of specified sets of inputs and outputs in the provision of healthcare between this system and traditional home health care. Inputs involve the level of medical expertise, facilities, technology, service personnel and client characteristics. The focus is on assessing the effects of known quantities of healthcare –such as episodes of care and hospital stays, etc. and examine those in relation to traditional care. If, for example, home based e-heath applications would increase costs and produce the same clinical outcomes as traditional homecare, they would have failed to address the challenges of home care. Cost savings from the use of e-health systems in home care can be realized if following outcomes can be demonstrated: a) reduction of unnecessary visits to the emergency room; b) prevention of repeat hospitalizations or in general, overall decrease of re-hospitalization rates; c) reduction of unnecessary/unscheduled visits to the physician's office; and d) patient education that leads to improvement of lifestyle choices and medication compliance.

6. Discussion

The health care sector struggles to restrict expenditures, and as a result, the emphasis is placed on outpatient services. Given the increase of life expectancy and the aging population, the number of patients being cared for at home is increasing. As home health care services become more costly and the problem of home health provider shortage is increasing, e-health technology can provide a cost-effective alternative providing quality care for rural and urban populations.

The first concept discussed in this paper was that of telehomecare. The use of telemedicine technologies introduces the notion of a virtual visit, an interaction between patient and health care provider separated by geographic distance. As this mode of care delivery is being introduced into the care plan, we have to examine the appropriate ways of integration of virtual visits. The type of virtual visit and the visit pattern itself should be determined by the health care provider based on the patient's primary diagnosis, stability and ability to use the system. Several factors must be considered when determining if use of technology is ethical and appropriate for a particular patient such as the patient's stability of disease processes, level of functional limitations, infrastructure at the patient's home (depending on the type of application, a phone line, a phone and/or a TV set might be required), the patients' mental state and their attitude towards the system and willingness to provide informed consent. The American Telemedicine Association [44] has produced a set of clinical guidelines for the development and deployment of telehomecare applications. These guidelines refer to patient, technology and provider criteria. Patient criteria involved a set of recommendations such as the need for informed written consent obtained from patients, selection of patients able to handle the equipment, and training. Technology criteria refer to the operation and maintenance of equipment, establishment of clear procedures and safety codes and protection of patient privacy and record security. Health provider criteria refer to training issues and after hours support.

The second concept, that of smart homes, refers to an innovative concept that places the technology within the residency in order to increase functionality, security and quality of life. A smart home enables non-obtrusive monitoring of residents and there are different levels of sophistication of the technology involved, ranging from stand-alone intelligent devices to homes that continuously monitor residents' activities and physical status and adopt to residents' needs, often providing proactive measures. The concept of smart homes is relatively new and we are still lacking an ethical framework for the design and implementation of such residencies. Moran [45] was one of the first to pose crucial questions about the social impact of smart technologies. She stated that

> *"The introduction of advanced technology into the home has the potential to change qualitative and quantitative aspects of relationships between household members, as well as the role and function of the home and its relationship with the wider environment. Such technologies consequently have important implications for our health and quality of life."*

In the context of smart homes, one needs to address the possibility of such technologies removing choice and control from the users as they learn to rely on automation. A further concern is that of transfer of personal information to third parties, without proper consent. Specifically, and in relation to the first concern, there are fears that smart homes may result in a reduction of social interaction, or may provide tools that substitute personal forms of care and communication [46,47]. Thus, it is important to consider when discussing the design of smart home applications the warning by Wyde and Valins [48] that we may be creating "societies of high tech hermits."

Electronic home healthcare systems can potentially redesign home care delivery. The premise of the use of technology in this field is that by bridging geographic distance and enabling distant monitoring, home care professionals can provide better quality of care through increased access to care, early detection and intervention, and patient involvement in the decision making and care process. E-health applications can increase patients' knowledge, autonomy, level of control and satisfaction with the delivered care services if technology is used appropriately [49] and stakeholders collaborate effectively [50, 51]. With technological advancements comes the desire to use such technology in all aspects of life; even in cases where such an implementation follows no framework or promotes outdated medical models that view users as dependant patients instead of enhancing their engagement, social inclusion and independence. The challenge as we create new technologies, is to understand the personal effects of the technology in order to make it better serve our human purposes.

References

[1] National association for home care (2000) 'Basic statistics about home care 2000', 18 March 2004, http://www.nahc.org/Consumer/hcstats.html

[2] How we are changing; the demographic state of the nation. Report P23-188. US Department of Commerce, Economics and Statistics Administration, Washington, DC: US Census Bureau; 1994

[3] Sparks, K.E., Shaw, D.K., Eddy, D., Hanigosky, P. and Vantrese, J. (1993) 'Alternatives for cardiac rehabilitation patients unable to return to a hospital based program' *Heart and Lung,* Vol. 22, pp.298-303.

[4] Turnin, M.C., Bolzonella-Pene, C., Dumoulin, S., Cerf, I., Charpentier, G. (1995) 'Multicenter evaluation of the Nutri-Expert Telemeatic System in diabetic patients' *Diabetes and Metabolism,* Vol.21, pp. 26-33.

[5] Friedman, R.H., Kazis, L.E., Jette, A., Smith, M.B., Stollerman, J., Torgerson, J. and Carey, K. (1996) 'A Telecommunications system for monitoring and counseling patients with hypertension: Impact on medication adherence and blood pressure control' *American Journal of Hypertension*, Vol.9, pp. 285-292.

[6] Johnston, B., Wheeler, L., Deuser, J. and Sousa, K.H. (2000) 'Outcomes of the Kaiser Permanent Tele-Home Health Research Project' *Archives of Family Medicine,* Vol. 9, pp.40-45.

[7] Finkelstein, J., O'Connor, G. and Friedmann, R.H. (2001) 'Development and implementation of the home asthma telemonitoring (HAT) system to facilitate asthma self-care' *MedInfo*, 10(Pt 1), pp. 810-814.

[8] Baker, A.M., Lafata, J.E., Ward, R.E., Whitehouse, F. and Divine, G. (2001) 'A web-based diabetes care management support system' *Joint Commission Journal on Quality Improvement*, Vol. 27, No.4, pp.179-190.

[9] Riva, A., Bellazzi, R. and Stefanelli, M. (1997) 'A Web-based system for the intelligent management of diabetic patients' *MD Computing*, Vol.14, No. 5, pp.360-364.

[10] Demiris, G., Speedie, S.M. and Finkelstein, S.M. (2001) The nature of communication in virtual home care visits. *Proceedings of the American Medical Informatics Association Symposium*, pp. 135-138.

[11] Jerant AF, Azari R, Nesbitt T. Reducing the Cost of Frequent Hospital Admissions for Congestive Heart Failure. *Medical Care* 2001;39 (11):1234-1245.

[12] Riegel B et al. Effect of a Standardized Nurse Case Management Telephone Intervention on Resource Use in Patients with Chronic Heart Failure. *Arch Int Medicine* 2002;162:705-712.

[13] Poon WS, Leuing CHS, Kan MK, Wal CP. The comparative impact of video-consultation on neurosurgical health services. *Internationl Journal of Medical Informatics* 2000;162:175-180.

[14] Dansky K, Palmer L, Shea D, Boles K. Cost-Analysis of Telehomecare. *Telemedicine Journal and e-Health* 2001; 7(3):225-232.

[15] de Lusignan S. Wells S. Johnson P. Meredith K. Leatham E. Compliance and effectiveness of 1 year's home telemonitoring. The report of a pilot study of patients with chronic heart failure. *European Journal of Heart Failure* 2001 3(6):723-30.

[16] Dansky K, Boles K. Lessons learned from a telehomecare project. *Caring* 2002; (April): 18-22.

[17] Doolittle G. A Cost Measurement for a Home-Based Telehospice Service. *Journal of Telemedicine and Telecare* 2000;6 Suppl 1:S

[18] Bai J, Zhang Y, Shen D, Wen L, et al. A portable ECG and blood pressure telemonitoring system. *IEEE Eng Med Biol Mag* 1999;18(4):63-70.

[19] Barbaro V, Bartolini P, Bernarducci R. A portable unit for remote monitoring of pacemaker patients. *Journal of Telemedicine and Telecare* 1997;3(2):96-102.

[20] Dahlberg NL, Blazek D, Wikoff B, Tuckwell BL, Koloroutis M. High-tech, high-touch perinatal home care. *Caring* 1995;14(5):36-9.

[21] University of Wollongong (2001) 'Intelligent Knee to Save Costly Sporting Injuries', November 10th, http://www.uow.edu.au/science/research/ipri/kneesleeve.html

[22] Lynch, A., Diamond, D. and Leader, M. (2000) 'Point-of-Need Diagnosis of Cystic Fibrosis Using a Potentiometric Ion-Selective Electrode Array' *Analyst,* Vol. 125, No.12, pp. 2264–2267.

[23] Tamada, J.A., Garg, S., Jovanovic, L., Pitzer, K.R., Fermi, S. and Potts RO. (1999) 'Non-Invasive Glucose Monitoring: Comprehensive Clinical Results' *Journal of the American Medical Association,* Vol. 282, No. 19, pp.1839–1844.

[24] Wahr, J.A., Tremper, K.K. (1995) 'Non-Invasive Oxygen Monitoring Techniques' *Critical Care Clinics,* Vol.11, No.1, pp.199–217.

[25] Georgia Institute of Technology (2003) 'Smart Shirt Moves from Research to Market', 18 March 2004, http://www.gatech.edu/news-room/archive/news_releases/sensatex.html

[26] Elger, G. and Furugren, B. (1998) 'SmartBo-an ICT and computer based demonstration home for disabled people', Proceedings 3rd TIDE Congress: Technology for Inclusive Design and Equality Improving the Quality of Life for the European Citizen, Helskinki, Finland.

[27] Chan, M., Bocquet, H., Campo, E., Val, T. and Pous, J. (1999) 'Alarm communication network to help carers of the elderly for safety purposes: a survey of a project' International Journal of Rehabilitation Research, Vol. 22, pp.131-136.

[28] Chan, M., Bocquet, H. and Steenkeste, F. (1999) 'Remote monitoring system for the assessment of noctural behavioral disorders in the demented' *European Medical and Biological Engineering Conference EMBEC*, Vienna, Austria.

[29] Kidd, C.D., Orr, R.J., Abowd, G.D. and Atkeson, C.G. (1999) 'The Aware Home: A Living Laboratory for Ubiquitous Computing Research', *Proceedings of the Second International Workshop on Cooperative Buildings, CoBuild.*

[30] Aldrich FL. Smart Homes: Past, Present and Future. In Richard Harper (ed.) Inside the Smart Home Springer Verlag 2003, p. 34-35

[31] Telecommunications Industry Association (2003) 'Resource guide for accessible design of consumer electronics-linking product design to the needs of people with functional limitations: a joint venture of the electronic industries alliance and the electronic industries foundations', 18 March 2004, http://www.tiaonline.org/access/guide.html

[32] Bellazzi, R., Montani, S., Riva, A. and Stefanelli, M. (2001) 'Web-based telemedicine systems for home-care: technical issues and experiences' *Computer methods and programs in biomedicine*, Vol. 64, No.3, pp.175-187.

[33] Demiris, G., Finkelstein, S.M. and Speedie, S.M. (2001) 'Considerations for the design of a Web-based clinical monitoring and educational system for elderly patients' *Journal of the American Medical Informatics Association*, Vol. 8, No. 5, pp. 468-472.

[34] U.S. Department of Health and Human Services. Office of the Secretary Standards for privacy of individually identifiable health information; proposed rule. Fed Regist 1999 Nov 3;64(212):59917-60016

[35] O'Conaill, B.O. (1997) 'Characterizing, predicting, and measuring video-mediated communication: a conversational approach', in K E Finn and A. J. Sellen, (eds.), *Video-Mediated Communication*, Erlbaum, Mahwah, NJ, pp. 107–131.

[36] Street, R.L., Jr. (1992) 'Communicative styles and adaptations in physician-parent consultations.' *Social Science and Medicine*, Vol.34, pp.1155-1163.

[37] Ende, J., Kazis, L., Ash, A. and Moskowitz, MA.(1989) 'Measuring patients' desire for autonomy: Decision-making and information-seeking preferences among medical patients' *Journal of General Internal Medicine*, Vol.4, pp. 23-30.

[38] Lerman, C., Brody, D.S., Caputo, G.C., Smith, D.G., Lazaro, C.G. and Wolfson, H.G. (1990) Perceived involvement in care scale: Relationship to attitudes about illness and medical care. *Journal of General Internal Medicine*, Vol. 5, pp. 29-33.

[39] Rost, K.M., Carter, W. and Inui, T. (1989) 'Introduction of information during the initial medical visit: Consequences for patient follow-through with physician recommendations for medication' *Social Science and Medicine*, Vol. 28, pp: 315-321.

[40] Street, R.L. Jr. and Voigt, B. (1997) 'Patient participation in deciding breast cancer treatment and subsequent quality of life' *Medical Decision Making*, Vol. 17, pp.298-306.

[41] Kaplan, S.H., Greenfield, S. and Ware, JE Jr. (1989) 'Assessing the effects of physician-patient interactions on the outcomes of chronic disease' *Medical Care*, Vol. 27, pp.S110-S127.

[42] Bashshur, R.L.(1995) 'On the definition and evaluation of telemedicine' *Telemedicine Journal*, Vol.1, pp. 19-30.

[43] Demiris, G., Speedie, S.M. and Finkelstein, S.M. (2000) 'An instrument for the assessment of patients' impressions of the risks and benefits of home telecare' *Journal of Telemedicine and Telecare*, Vol. 6, pp.278-284.

[44] American Telemedicine Association (2003) 'ATA adopts Telehomecare Clinical Guidelines', 18 March 2004, http://www.americantelemed.org/icot/hometelehealthguidelines.htm

[45] Moran R. The electronic home: Social and spatial aspects. Dublin: European Foundation for the Improvement of Living and Working Conditions. 1993

[46] Dick S, Pomfret D. Community alarm systems study. Edinburgh" Age Concern Scotland 1996

[47] Tetley J, Hanson E, Clarke A. Older people, telematics and care in A. M. Warnes, L. Warren and M. Nolan (eds) Care services for later life: Transformations and critiques. London: Jessica Kingsley Publications, p. 243-258.

[48] Wylde M, Valins MS. "The impact of technology" in M.S. Valins and D. Salter (eds) Futurecare: New directions in planning health and care environments. Oxford: Blackwell Science, p. 15-24.

[49] O'Connor, S.J. and Lanning, J.A. (2001) 'Rehumanizing technology in healthcare delivery' *International Journal of Healthcare Technology and Management,* Vol. 3, pp. 26-33.

[50] Paul, D.L. (2000) 'Telemedicine: a virtual collaboration perspective' *International Journal of Healthcare Technology and Management*, Vol. 2, pp. 37-55.

[51] Rosenborg, L.D. (2003) 'A facilitated approach to developing collaborative action in primary healthcare' *International Journal of Healthcare Technology and Management*, Vol.5, pp. 63-80

E-Health: Current Status and Future Trends
G. Demiris (Ed.)
IOS Press, 2004

Mr. Young's Doctor: How Must Physicians Be Prepared for Practice?

Linda A. HEADRICK, M.D., M.S.
University of Missouri-Columbia, School of Medicine
USA

Abstract. What will the practice of medicine be like when people use publicly-available performance data to choose their physicians, own their own medical records and therefore exercise more control over medical decision making than has ever been seen in the past? What do these changes mean for the preparation of physicians? The Institute of Medicine has set forth six aims for health care in the United States, that it be safe, effective, patient-centered, timely, efficient and equitable. Achieving this requires new rules for our work in health care and new goals for medical education. The University of Missouri-Columbia School of Medicine has identified eight key characteristics of its graduating students and residents. We believe these are the qualities required for future physicians to deliver the care that their patients need and deserve.

Introduction

The purpose of this paper is to consider two questions. The first: What will the practice of medicine be like when people use publicly-available performance data to choose their physicians, own their own medical records and therefore exercise more control over medical decision making than has ever been seen in the past? All these changes are part of what health policy leaders in the United States think that health care should be like in the future, if we want a system that gives the care our patients need and deserve. [1]

The second: What do these changes mean for the preparation of physicians? Put another way, if this is the future, what should medical education be doing right now?

A Case

Let's look at the present and the future through the eyes of Richard Young, a 34-year-old architect who is married with two children. Mr. Young was born in Southeast Asia. He immigrated to the U.S. at age three with his aunt, who subsequently "Americanized" both their names. Mr. Young's parents were killed when he was an infant. Little is known about their health. After arriving in the U.S., Mr. Young was diagnosed with chronic hepatitis B virus infection (HBV), presumably acquired at birth. Throughout his life, Mr. Young's health has been good. He and his physicians have monitored the HBV closely; he has never received any treatment.

Mr. Young recently accepted a new job in a new city. One of his relocation tasks is to transfer his health care. After moving in, Mr. Young asks his new neighbor, a pharmacist, to recommend a primary care physician. Mr. Young makes an appointment with the person he recommends, Dr. Martin. The first visit is focused on reviewing the medical history. Mr. Young signs a release to obtain a copy of the old medical records. Dr. Martin refers Mr. Young to a liver specialist, Dr. Greenwood, for evaluation and follow-up of the HBV.

Two months later, at the consultation with Dr. Greenwood, Mr. Young discovers that the only information Dr. Greenwood has received is a brief letter from the referring physician, Dr. Martin. The clinic staff call Dr. Martin's office to inquire about old records. What they have is faxed over: two pages of blood work results from six and twelve months ago.

Mr. Young is appalled. He had seen his previous physician for fifteen years with blood work every six months. One year ago, they considered entering him into an antiviral drug trial, so a liver biopsy was done. None of this information is available now. Mr. Young signs another release for information, this time specifically requesting the liver biopsy results. At the end of the visit, Dr. Greenwood suggests that they consider another liver biopsy, "so that we'll have the tissue here."

Mr. Young is not very happy with all this. He has lived with HBV all his life. He knows a lot about it. In partnership with his previous physicians, he's been following research on antiviral treatment for people in his situation. Now he feels like he's starting all over again. He wonders what it will take to get his new doctors up to speed. Will he be able to convince them to take his needs and preferences into account as they make decisions about the future?

What Mr. Young's Care Could (and Should) Be Like

Let's roll back the tape and look at what Mr. Young's care could (and should) be like.

Before his move, Mr. Young visits a secure Web site and downloads an updated copy of his medical record. This includes visit notes, blood work results, digital images of a liver biopsy from one year ago, the pathologist's interpretation of the liver biopsy, and abstracts of recent papers Mr. Young and his physician discussed when they were trying to decide if he should enter a new antiviral drug trial.

Using the Web, Mr. Young reads about the health systems, primary care physicians and liver specialists in his new city. He looks at how they compare with regard to clinical outcomes for common conditions and patient satisfaction scores. The practice profile of one of the gastroenterology physicians, Dr. Greenwood, includes a fair number of patients with hepatitis B.

Mr. Young talks with his new neighbor, a pharmacist. The pharmacist confirms that Dr. Greenwood specializes in liver disease. He seems to be well-liked among his patients, who appear to be well-informed. The pharmacist also suggests two primary care physicians who are known for being good "team players," working well with multiple providers in caring for patients with chronic disease. As it turns out, all three of these physicians are part of a system that has invested heavily in information technology and offers patients open access to their medical records. The pharmacist considers this a big plus. Mr. Young agrees.

Mr. Young uses the health system's Web-based welcome system to make appointments with one of the recommended primary care physicians and with the liver specialist, Dr. Greenwood. He completes a pre-visit questionnaire, giving details of his history, and uploads his prior medical record.

At the first visit with Dr. Greenwood two weeks later, Mr. Young and Dr. Greenwood electronically pull up all of the information and review it together. Much of the visit is spent discussing the pros and cons of the antiviral drug trial. Mr. Young explains that in the process of considering this trial, he realized that he is a "leave well enough alone" kind of guy. As long as he feels well and his liver function studies remain normal, he just doesn't feel that drug therapy is worth the risks. Even if the virus clears initially, what's the possibility of recurrence when the drug is stopped? What's the risk of drug resistance? Why not wait until his clinical status suggests a need for drug therapy?

Since there is no evidence to support drug therapy over watchful waiting for patients like Mr. Young, Dr. Greenwood supports Mr. Young's decision (although he notes that a patient he saw yesterday decided on exactly the opposite course). They agree to continue with twice yearly monitoring of blood work. They also agree that given the data from the previous liver biopsy, there is no need for invasive testing, like a repeat liver biopsy, unless something changes.

After returning home, Mr. Young visits the health system Web site again and goes to the "library," as recommended by a nurse at Dr. Greenwood's practice. He signs up to receive electronic notices of publications related to HBV. However, he declines the opportunity to join an electronic patient support group; he doesn't feel it's worth the time right now.

Can We Have a Health Care System That Will Do All This?

In 2001, the Institute of Medicine (IOM) released a landmark report, Crossing the Quality Chasm. [1] It was very critical of health care in the U.S, citing study after study of underuse, overuse and misuse of medical care. The conclusion was that the gap between what we know as best care and what we are able to deliver everyday is not just a gap, it's a *chasm*. However, the report overall was optimistic and positive. It expressed a belief that Americans could "have a health care system of the quality they need, want and deserve... This level of quality cannot be achieved by further stressing current systems of care. The current systems cannot do the job. Trying harder will not work. Changing systems of care will." [1]

The IOM Chasm report set forth six aims for health care in the U.S: safe, effective, patient-centered, timely, efficient and equitable.

- *Safe*: Avoiding injuries to patients from the care that is intended to help them.
- *Effective*: Avoiding underuse and overuse: providing services based on scientific knowledge to all who could benefit and refraining from providing services to those not likely to benefit.
- *Patient-centered:* Providing care that is respectful and responsive to individual patient preferences, needs, and values and ensuring that patient values guide all clinical decisions.
- *Timely*: Reducing waits and sometimes harmful delays for both those who receive and those who give care.
- *Efficient*: Avoiding waste, including waste of equipment, supplies, ideas and energy.
- *Equitable:* Providing care that does not vary in quality because of personal characteristics such as gender, ethnicity, and socioeconomic status.

To help us get there the IOM report suggested ten rules for redesigning and improving care.[1] They were labeled "ten simple rules." (Table 1) They may be simple in concept, but the implications for health care are profound.

Table 1. New Rules to Redesign and Improve Care

1. Care based on continuous healing relationships. 2. Customization based on patient needs and values. 3. The patient as the source of control. 4. Shared knowledge and free flow of information 5. Evidence-based decision making 6. Safety as a system property 7. Need for transparency 8. Anticipation of needs 9. Continuous decrease in waste 10. Cooperation among clinicians
From the Institute of Medicine, 2001

Let's briefly review these, comparing our old assumptions about care to these new rules. Then we'll consider what this means for educating new physicians.

Rule #1: Care based on continuous healing relationships
(Current assumption: Care based on visits)

In the current way, care is based on face-to-face visits. Patient and physician or other health care provider meet together in an exam or procedure room. This face-to-face care is the basis for most third-party payment. Phone calls, emails and other methods of communication are extra. They may be expected, but the time spent usually is not scheduled or compensated.

The IOM believes that care should be based on continuous relationships instead of visits. This means all sorts of interactions that improve the transfer of information and strengthen the healing relationship: patient access to scheduling, medical records, and email communications with their providers; on-line support of self-care with education, access to scientific information, and electronic discussion groups; and health care delivery in multiple forms, including Telehealth consultations. Face-to-face visits continue to be important, but they are only a part of the care given in the context of this continuous relationship.

This approach may improve the efficiency and quality of face-to-face time. Consider Mr. Young's case. The efficiency and quality of his visit with Dr. Greenwood was enhanced greatly by the fact that the transfer of information occurred beforehand (a pre-visit questionnaire, electronic transfer of the previous medical record). During the precious time that Mr. Young and Dr. Greenwood met face-to-face, the review of background information was completed quickly. They spent most of their time discussing issues pertinent to the decisions they needed to make together.

Rule #2: Customization based on patient needs and values
(Current assumption: Professional autonomy drives variability)

Studies over the past several years have shown that the time-honored value of professional autonomy may lead to differences in practice that are not always consistent with current evidence, resulting in different outcomes for similar patients. [2,3] This new rule agrees that variation in treatment should be present, but should be driven by differences in patient needs, preferences and values.

It's our job to ensure that each patient has the best available information about applying what we know to his or her individual circumstance. Then we must work together to agree on a path forward.

Mr. Young has every right to expect knowledge and use of the same medical evidence regardless of where he receives care. He also should expect individualization of care according to his needs, preferences and values. Where there is no clear answer from the literature (like whether or not patients with asymptomatic chronic HBV should be on antiviral drug therapy), variation should depend on each patient's judgment of the benefits and risks.

Rule #3: The patient as the source of control
(Current assumption: Professionals control care)

In the current system, the professionals control care. Patients often must have permission to see their own medical record or have family present at critical times. Under this new rule, the patient is the source of control, except in unusual circumstances (like a medical emergency, when patient is unable to make decisions). The literature tells us that most patients want to be involved in treatment decisions and to know about alternatives. [4,5] We are learning that informed patients participating actively have better outcomes, lower costs and higher functional status. [6-7] This does not mean that patients should be forced to share decision making; only that they should be able to exercise the degree of control that they wish.

Rule #4: Shared knowledge and free flow of information
(Current assumption: Information is a record)

Currently, information about care is primarily a record of the patient visit. It is not interactive and often there are barriers to information transfer (like in Mr. Young's case). Under the new rule, the transfer of information is a key part of care. Both personal and scientific information should be easily and routinely available. As mentioned earlier, there is growing evidence that this approach can improve health outcomes.

Rule #5: Evidence-based decision making
(Current assumption: Decision making is based on training and experience)

We've already talked about the variations in outcomes of care that can result when best evidence is not used. One hundred years ago, the doctor's own experience may have been the best source of information for what to do. Now we have the opportunity to make our decision-making much more evidence-based. When clinicians have access to evidence-based analyses like those done by the Cochrane Collaboration [8-9], they can focus their experience and judgment on those choices that science cannot guide.

Rule #6: Safety as a system property
(Current assumption: Do no harm is an individual responsibility)

Many health professionals have been trained with the unstated but powerful assumption that careful and competent professionals do not and should not make errors. If errors occur, it was because someone was not knowledgeable enough, caring enough, or didn't try hard enough.

In reality, errors will occur, no matter how smart, careful or hard-working we are. Errors are the end result of complex interactions between the systems in which we work and human factors such as fatigue and distraction. There is a limit to what individual humans can do to improve safety. Significant gains require systems that are designed to prevent error and to mitigate harm when error occurs. [10] That is, to make it easy to do the right thing and hard to do the wrong.

Rule #7: Need for transparency
(Current assumption: Secrecy is necessary)

Our current system works under the assumption that secrecy is necessary. It wasn't that long ago that we routinely withheld information to "protect" patients from knowledge felt to be potentially upsetting or harmful.[5] It is still the norm that we keep secrets to protect ourselves from possible litigation.

The IOM argues that transparency is necessary to achieving the six aims in health care. Information must flow freely so that everyone, including patients and families, can make informed choices. A system that operates under a rule of transparency will be safer because anyone (including patients) will be able to recognize outdated or wrong information and share information that affects their care.

This is a tough one, given the malpractice environment in the United States. But some health care systems have taken this on and claim that open error disclosure has decreased their total malpractice burden. The number of claims may increase, but the total dollar amount is smaller because of early disclosure and aggressive intervention to mitigate or compensate harm.

Rule #8: Anticipation of needs
(Current assumption: The system reacts to needs)

One sage noted that we should "quit being surprised" when people want to see us when they are sick. We can use predictive models to anticipate demand and allocate resources accordingly, smoothing workflow, increasing efficiency and improving the work environment. We can use patient registries to track patient needs and draw them into care, not just wait until they show up at the door. There is evidence that such an approach for high risk patients with chronic disease can improve care, decrease costs and improve quality of life. [11]

Rule #9: Continuous decrease in waste
(Current assumption: Cost reduction is sought)

There is a major problem with health care costs in the U.S. The current approach to dealing with increasing costs is to restrict services, limit budgets, and create barriers to care. The IOM argues that our approach to decreasing cost should be to attack waste. That means removing expenditures that add no value.

Think about the waste in the first version of Mr. Young's story. Professional time was spent gathering information that someone else had already compiled. Clinic staff spent time and energy seeking the old record. There was even a suggestion that an expensive and invasive procedure be repeated because of the inability to get previous results in a timely manner.

Rule #10: Cooperation among clinicians
(Current assumption: Preference is given to professional roles over the system)

Currently, each discipline tends to defend its authority and independence, often at the cost of effective collaboration. As a result, patients experience poor communication and waste. How many times have we heard from patients, "Don't you guys talk to each other?" To achieve our goals in care, we need good communication among all the members of the health care team, bringing to the patient whatever expertise and knowledge are required to meet the need.

What Does This Mean for the Preparation of New Physicians?

Over the past year at the University of Missouri-Columbia School of Medicine, in a set of activities labeled "MU 2020," we've taken a serious look at the future of health care and the implications for the preparation of new physicians.[1] We learned what we could about the anticipated health needs and practice of medicine in the year 2020. We then asked ourselves, "What do our graduates need to be like to practice successfully in the future?"

The result is a list of eight key characteristics of our medical school and residency graduates. (Table 2) These are the foundation for updated educational goals and refined evaluation strategies. We want to be able to say to a potential student or resident, "If you come here for your education, this is the kind of physician you'll become and here's how we will know."

Table 2. MU 2020 Key Characteristics of Graduating Students and Residents.

1. Able to deliver effective patient-centered care 2. Honest with high ethical standards 3. Knowledgeable in biomedical sciences, evidence-based practice, and societal and cultural issues 4. Critical thinker; problem-solver 5. Able to communicate with patients and others 6. Able to collaborate with patients and other members of health care team 7. Committed to improving quality and safety 8. Committed to life-long learning and information mastery
University of Missouri-Columbia School of Medicine, 2003

Table 3 shows how the MU 2020 key characteristics are consistent with the Accreditation Council for Graduate Medical Education (ACGME) core competencies. [12] Since 2003, accredited residency programs in the U.S. must demonstrate that their

[1] The author wishes to acknowledge the University of Missouri School of Medicine MU 2020 Steering Committee and numerous other faculty, students and staff for their work on this initiative. They are the authors of the work described here.

graduates are competent in these areas. Supporting our residencies in the MU 2020 key characteristics will help them achieve the ACGME core competencies.

Table 3. ACGME Competencies compared to MU 2020 Key Characteristics

ACGME COMPETENCIES	MU 2020 KEY CHARACTERISTICS
1. Patient Care	Effective patient-centered care
2. Medical Knowledge	Knowledgeable in biomedical sciences, evidence-based practice, and societal and cultural issues Critical thinker; problem-solver
3. Practice-based learning and improvement	Committed to improving quality and safety Committed to life-long learning and information mastery
4. Interpersonal and communication skills	Able to communicate with patients and others
5. Professionalism	Honest with high ethical standards
6. Systems-based practice	Able to collaborate with patients and other members of the health care team

Able to deliver effective patient-centered care

First and foremost, we seek to graduate physicians who are able to deliver patient-centered care. That means care that reflects respect for individual patient values, preferences, and expressed needs. It must be grounded in the best available evidence and conserve limited resources. Patient-centered care depends on shared decision-making and active patient participation. It is marked by compassion, empathy and patient advocacy.

Honest with high ethical standards

We seek to graduate physicians whose work reflects honesty in relationships with patients, colleagues and the societal systems designed to support health care. They must understand and adhere to the basic principles of medical ethics including justice, beneficence, non-maleficence, and respect for patient autonomy.

Knowledgeable in biomedical sciences, evidence-based practice, and societal and cultural issues

Future physicians must possess a fund of knowledge that reflects the current understandings in basic biomedical sciences, evidence-based practice in the clinical disciplines, and social and cultural issues that impact patient care. This is an essential part of the foundation for good care.

Critical thinker; problem-solver

Having a good knowledge base is important, but it isn't enough. The physician of the future needs to be a critical thinker and problem-solver, to be able to process and modify information, and to be able to apply available knowledge to individual patient need. We also want our graduates to be intellectually curious and to question the status quo. Asking "Why can't it be better?" is the first step toward building new knowledge and improvements in care.

Able to communicate with patients and others

Future physicians must demonstrate competence in verbal and nonverbal communication skills with patients, families and health care providers. Think about the IOM goals and rules for health care in the future. They are all about partnership and shared decision making. That requires communication. Our graduates must be able to establish professional, caring relationships and to facilitate the delivery of high quality, compassionate patient-centered health care.

Able to collaborate with patients and other members of health care team

Facilitating high quality patient-centered care means being part of a team. That requires mutual cooperation, respect, exchange of information and meaning, sharing resources, and enhancing each other's capacity for mutual benefits. Recently we did an experiment in our curriculum. Senior nursing students, graduate students in health administration, and pharmacy residents joined second year medical students in a two-hour learning experience on patient safety. The students were assembled into interdisciplinary teams that analyzed cases of medical error in a modified root cause analysis. Afterwards, at least a half dozen medical students came up to say, "We need more of this," meaning opportunities to learn about and with other health professionals.

Committed to improving quality and safety

Physicians must also be able to work as members of the health care team to strive for excellence in the quality of patient care and safety. That means assessing the results of current practice, analyzing the literature to determine best practice, and taking action to close any gaps. [13] They must be able to recognize their own limitations as humans working in an imperfect system and work to prevent hazards in delivering health care. The University of Missouri-Columbia is a founding member of a 12-school collaborative dedicated to integrating learning about quality and safety into the core medical school curriculum. [14]

Committed to life-long learning and information mastery

Finally, we believe our graduates must be committed to self-assessment and improvement. Physicians must be able to continually appraise and assimilate scientific evidence to keep abreast of changes in medical knowledge and practice. That means knowing the basics of how information is organized, being able to access it effectively, synthesizing pertinent information and communicating the knowledge gained. In medical school, all we can do is help them get started. Knowledge will change dramatically between now and the year 2020, when many of the Class of 2004 will be at the peak of their practice.

What is Next?

At the University of Missouri-Columbia School of Medicine, we are in the process of moving from these eight key characteristics to a revised set of overall learning goals for the medical school curriculum. Key to reaching these goals is an integrated evaluation strategy: "If you come here for your education, this is the kind of physician you'll become and here's how we will know."

We also are nearing completion of a set of design principles for the educational experiences themselves. These principles will help us model the behaviors we seek for our graduates. Our goal as educators is to be learner-centered, honest with high ethical standards, knowledgeable, critical thinkers and problem-solvers, good communicators, good collaborators, committed to continuously improving the quality of the education experience and committed to life-long learning.

We want our graduates to be the kind of doctor that Mr. Young was seeking. They will be ready to help build the kind of health care system that all of our patients need and deserve.

References

[1] Institute of Medicine. Crossing the Quality Chasm: A New Health System for the 21st Century. Washington DC: National Academy Press, 2001.

[2] Dartmouth Medical School Center for the Evaluative Clinical Sciences. The Dartmouth Atlas of Health Care. Chicago, Ill. : American Hospital Publishing, 1999.

[3] Fisher ES. Medical care--is more always better?[comment]. New England Journal of Medicine. 349(17):1665-7, 2003 Oct 23.

[4] Stewart M, Brown JB, Weston WW, McWhinney IR et al. Patient-Centered Medicine: Transforming the Clinical Method. 2nd edition. Oxon UK:Radcliffe Medical Press, 2003.

[5] Buckman R. How to Break Bad News: A Guide for Health Professionals. Baltimore: The Johns Hopkins University Press, 1992.

[6] Stewart S, Brown JB, Donner A, McWhinney IR et al. The Impact of Patient-Centered Care on Outcomes. J Family Practice. 2000;49:796-804.

[7] Kaplan SH, Greenfield S, Ware JE. Assessing the Effects of Physician-Patient Interactions on Outcomes of Chronic Disease. Medical Care. 1989;27(3, Supplement):S110-27.

[8] Levin A. The Cochrane Collaboration. Annals of Internal Medicine. 2001;135:309-12.

[9] The Cochrane Collaboration. http://www.cochrane.org/index0.htm.

[10] Leape LL. Error in Medicine. JAMA 1994;272:1851-1857.

[11] Chen A, Brown R, Archibald N, Aliotta S, Fox PD. Best Practices in Coordinated Care. Baltimore, MD: Health Care Financing Administration, 2000.

[12] Accreditation Council for Graduate Medical Education. Outcome Project. http://www.acgme.org/outcome/project/proHome.asp.

[13] Medical School Objectives Project. Report V. Contemporary Issues in Medicine: Quality of Care. Washington, D.C.:Association of American Medical Colleges, 2001.

[14] Griner G. Presentation to the Association of American Medical Colleges Council of Deans. Washington, D.C., April 2003.

E-Health: Current Status and Future Trends
G. Demiris (Ed.)
IOS Press, 2004

E-Health Tools and Social Workers

Debra PARKER OLIVER, MSW, PhD[1], George DEMIRIS, PhD[2]
[1]*School of Social Work, University of Missouri, Columbia*
[2]*School of Medicine, University of Missouri, Columbia*
USA

Abstract. Social workers have been using telemedicine technologies since the late 1950's. The use of telemedicine has been most common in mental health practice. Psychotherapy using telephones, interactive video and more recently the Internet have gained in popularity with social workers in these settings. However, the use of e-health tools in medical social work is limited and worthy of further investigation. This paper will report promising projects with medical social workers and discuss the potential application of e-health tools for these practitioners. The purpose of the paper is to advocate for research measuring effectiveness of e-health interventions in social work practice.

What is a social worker? What is the role of a medical social worker? These are classic questions that have plagued the profession. Stereotypically social workers are often thought of as those who work with the poor and disadvantaged, or perhaps as individuals whose purpose is either to hand out welfare, or take it away, depending on the perspective. The National Association of Social Workers Code of Ethics [1] defines social work as a profession with the primary mission to:

> ...enhance human well-being and help meet the basic human needs of all people, with particular attention to the needs and empowerment of people who are vulnerable, oppressed, and living in poverty. A historic and defining feature of social work is the profession's focus on individual well-being in a social context and the well-being of society. Fundamental to social work is attention to the environmental forces that create, contribute to, and address problems in living (p1).

Social work in a health care setting, known as medical social work, involves linking the social needs of individuals to their specific health care conditions. *The Social Work Dictionary* [2] identifies the purpose of medical social work as assisting physically ill clients and their families in resolving the social and psychological problems related to disease and illness. This includes assessment or diagnosis, goal establishment, intervention, methods and referral [3]. New electronic tools and media, e-health tools, are emerging for medical social workers as they provide these traditional services as well as new ones to their patients. While these activities have been carried out with traditional means and during face-to-face interactions, new electronic tools and media are emerging for medical social workers to assist with the delivery of these and new services. Many believe that e-health tools can revolutionize the field of social work.

e-Health is defined as the use of advanced telecommunications such as the Internet, portable and other sophisticated devices, advanced networks and new design approaches aiming to support healthcare delivery and education. Consequently, to reach the full potential of e-health a fundamental redesign of healthcare processes based on the use and integration of electronic communication at all levels is required. For medical social workers, e-health has the potential to facilitate patient empowerment, transitioning from a passive role where the patient is the recipient of care services to an active role where the patient is informed, has choices and is involved in the decision making process. e-Health bridges the clinical and non clinical sectors and includes both individual and population health-oriented tools. It encompasses different applications and concepts such as telemedicine applications that aim to bridge geographic distance using video-and audio-devices, web sites, online services for patient support groups, medical advice and diagnosis, consumer information services and portable monitoring tools that transmit physiological data to a central server. e-Health delivers healthcare information, diagnosis, treatment, and care in a nonlinear manner where traditional hierarchies are obsolete, and patients enter the system at an infinite number of points choosing their own terms of usage frequency and pattern.

While the use of technology in social work practice has historical roots and is gaining popularity, the concept of e-health is still quite new in the profession, and the use of e-health technologies is still rare [4]. Technology in social work is not yet commonly tied to the concepts of *e-health* or *e-learning*. In an Ovid search (in February 2004) of the databases from Medline, CINAL, PsychInfo, and SocioFile using the keywords "e-health", 294 references were found. Using the same databases and the key word "telemedicine" 4,962 references were identified. However, using the search words "social work" and "e-health" did not uncover a single reference, and using the terms "social work" and "telemedicine" found only 9 references. When using the traditional social work database, Social Work Abstracts, and the same keyword strategy, no references were identified. This literature search indicates that the terminology of social work and informatics are not yet linked and identifies opportunities in both professions for collaboration.

This chapter seeks to examine the state of the use of e-health technologies in social work practice and explore promising new trends. Additionally, the chapter will discuss the current controversies that exist related to the use of technology in practice. Finally, keys to the future use of e-health technology within social work will be identified and discussed.

The current state of technology use in Social Work

Mental health social workers were the first to utilize telemedicine in practice. As early as the1950's the profession was using interactive video for therapy [5]. However, these early innovations did not spread rapidly. The fear of technology and hesitations of social workers to adapt it is documented in social work history [6]. As early as 1911, Richmond, author of one of the first social work textbooks, writes of the importance of the telephone to social workers, encouraging its use, and recognizing the fears of practitioners related to the technology [6]. More recently, social work literature has identified the emergence of technology as a major trend affecting the future of the profession [7].

Current technologies are used by social workers in various arenas; with clients and colleagues, as well as agencies and communities. The use of technology in social work has been identified with four overarching purposes: 1) communication 2) assessment and treatment of clients 2) management of information 3) education [8, 9]. Documented uses of technology in social work are varied and involve telephone groups[10], mobile phones and facsimiles [8]. Additionally, online discussion groups, bulleting boards, online counseling and therapy [4, 5, 11], establishment of client and agency databases for information management and decision support [12-14]have emerged. Finally, technology applications have gained popularity in the education of college students and the training of practitioners [15].

Communication

As mentioned previously, as early as 1911 social work pioneers were advocating the telephone as a tool for intervention. The telephone has since been deemed a legitimate way to provide individual counseling services [16]. However, simple and obvious the effectiveness of this tool appears to be, research on its effectiveness for social work therapists and clients remains an empirical question [16]. One of the few published outcome studies assessing the effectiveness of communication technology was in rural Australia. The project evaluated the use of several technologies for individuals with disabilities living in remote areas. The findings indicate that practitioners adopted mobile phones and facsimiles for their practice easily [8]. The technology was credited with helping isolated practitioners keep in touch with their agency and clients. [8]. The focus of this research, however, was on the usefulness of the technology for the workers, rather than on outcomes for clients.

One survey of practitioners who had used computer and telephone interventions for group interventions found that these tools had great relevance for social work practice in health care [10]. Social Workers identified the benefits of increased availability of services to those who may not otherwise be willing or able to attend groups. Additionally, there is a cost savings for these groups as the expense and logistical difficulties of transportation is eliminated and no office space is required [10]. While holding great promise for social work with groups, there are unique leadership challenges to this practice and a need to construct a conceptual framework for it [17].

Client assessment and treatment

The use of the Internet for online individual assessment and counseling is growing in popularity. Online counseling has been defined as the delivery of therapeutic services using Internet applications that allow clients to receive services without face-to-face contact [18]. Use of the Internet with groups and communities has also been popular. Nartz researched the use of the Internet by community practice social workers. The project identified the Internet as most useful for practitioners for presenting information and communicating with others via email. The least useful reports were for newsgroups and chat discussions [19], nevertheless, a forum gaining momentum among practitioners involves the use of the Internet to link clients together in support groups.

One experimental study looked at the value of online support groups, using social workers as the research sample. This study found that short term, listserv-based groups function best if they have approximately 12 members. They also found that some members are more active than others, just as a traditional face-to-face group, and some members can dominate discussions while others are quiet. Additionally, they found leadership of online groups requires similar skills as traditional group work facilitation. Most group members in this study found the online group did provide the support for which they were hoping [20].

Data Management

Computers have changed management of social service agencies. Computerization and development of databases and systems allow for the organization, standardization, decision making support, and measurement of agency practice in new and diverse ways [12]. Databases are commonly used to hold information on clients, including health status and medical information. These databases are now critical in office management, including such functions as client tracking, billing, budgeting, and reporting.

A recent project has shown that computers can also assist with the case management of clients and the coordination of care. McCoy and Vila used computer technology to support a multi-site project to coordinate referrals [14]. They found that the capacity to track, verify, and standardize referrals had benefits to all organizations and their clients. This project resulted substantial increases in the referrals to all sites, standardization of referral data, and increased teamwork between providers. It was concluded that technology has tremendous potential to improve care coordination and health status of clients [14].

Education

Use of various technologies for learning is now common within the profession as distance education has gained in popularity and numerous studies have been published on the process, success, and limitation of these various technologies as compared to classrooms [21, 22]. Distance education research has found that numerous types of social work courses are effective using computer and online technology, including but not limited to practice courses[23], research methods [21], diversity [24], policy [22], and community practice [25] curriculum. Technology and related research have included computer simulations, Internet based coursework, streaming videoconferencing, interactive television, and others. All indications show that the use of these e-learning tools has been valuable to social work education and the delivery of coursework to students unable to attend a traditional college campus setting. It can be speculated that as more social workers are educated using the tools of technology, the technological skills and receptiveness to use of these tools will improve, thus leading to more practitioners choosing to integrate these new intervention methods into their clinical setting.

Promising e-health tools for the future

Four potential uses of the Internet in social work practice and treatment have been identified. These uses include extending the spectrum of services offered to clients regardless of location, the ability to provide factual, up to date, information and education to clients around the world, the possibility of linking individuals with similar issues together through online support groups, and tremendous training opportunities for professionals [26]. The potential ways to use the numerous technological tools emerging in today's world is nearly unlimited. This section identifies some recent innovations.

Borrowing from elementary education suggestions for email use in supplemental supervision, one social work author identified the Internet as one way to address access to supervision and consultations, a problem for many social workers, especially in isolated rural areas [27]. Additionally she explores the use of list serves and electronic bulletin boards, Internet conferences, and chat room discussions, as opportunities for professional discussion and networking [27]. All of these tools offer social workers unlimited methods to increase communication with one another.

In an attempt to help hospice workers communicate with their patients, the Missouri Tele-hospice Project is working on two promising uses for technology applicable to social work practice [28]. The first involves the use of PDA (personal digital assistants) technology for social work assessment. In this project the social worker uses a PDA to gather information on the anxiety and quality of life for caregivers of hospice patients. Initial and ongoing visit assessments are "tapped" into the PDA using the dropdown choices on the touch-screen. These notes are hot-synced into a computer, allowing for an ongoing comparison of caregiver psychosocial issues throughout the dying process.

The utilization of PDA's by social workers within the Missouri Telehospice Project is motivated by evidence that computerized patient surveys offer numerous advantages over traditional paper surveys when used by other professional groups. Advantages include increased efficiency of administration, reduction of data entry errors, improved ability to solicit sensitive or confidential information, elimination of paper storage and the potential for automatic scoring and report generation [29-31]. The project aims to determine whether computerized survey technology can provide an efficient and desirable method for social workers to collect data directly from patients or their caregivers. This technology holds great promise for a convenient, standardized assessment method for social work and other hospice professionals.

Secondly, the Missouri Tele-hospice Project proposes to use videophones in the homes of hospice patients. Videophones, using standard POTS (plain old telephone system) lines connect to similar phones in the hospice office. These videophones allow for audio and video contact between providers and patients, without a burden or stress of complicated, specialized equipment. Although similar initiatives have been tried before, the focus of previous work has been to save visits and cut costs for services [11]. This project does not seek to substitute virtual video visits for traditional visits, but rather enhance services through the addition of supplemental virtual visits and in times of crisis. In addition, it is hoped the videophone technology will allow the entire hospice team intervention and assessment opportunities as caregivers have the opportunity to enter into the traditional hospice team care plan meetings and participate as a member of the hospice team. Finally, an important difference in this project is that the social workers will be managing the study and utilizing the technology, which was previously the role of the nurse case manager [11]. The focus of the videophone intervention in this project is on the psychosocial issues of the patients and caregivers. It is hypothesized that the introduction of videophone technology will lower caregiver anxiety and thus improves the quality of their life.

Another promising use of videophone technology was recently demonstrated in an Assisted Living facility. Virginia-based Summerville Senior Living offers videophones to residents, family, and friends in their facility. The home has a community system involving a camera hooked to a TV and a telephone. Distant family members pay a fee for a unit to be mailed to them, allowing the resident and loved one the ability to interact and have a virtual family visit [32]. Social workers in long term care facilities, hospitals, and home care programs should consider this option, especially as the burden of distance, and stress of missing loved ones impact patient's medical conditions. This service offers the opportunity to have family conferences, and family involvement in plans of care in ways that might otherwise not be possible.

Recent research demonstrates the potential of a new intervention strategy- Internet Bibliotherapy. Bibliotherapy involves reading of supportive material, usually stories related to a client's situation. It may take two forms, interactive or self-help [33]. A recent narrative analysis of a biotherapy website of 22 cases indicated that clients experienced great support from the site. This study concluded that Internet Bibliotherapy has the potential to be both a valuable interactive and a self-help tool to be used as an adjunct with medical treatments [34].

The Internet, and other e-health tools currently and potentially available, will challenge social workers to re-conceptualize their practice, reframe their vision of the profession, and retrain themselves to understand the various technological tools. New tools require new standards to assure their appropriate use. Regardless of the purpose of the technology, the intended audience, or the means of the intervention, technology in social work is currently laden with controversy, all which must be taken into account.

Controversy within the profession

While the use of technology within social work practice is not a new concept, it is a controversial one. For a discipline traditionally tied to face-to-face interaction, many concerns about moving to technology based practices have been raised [35, 36]. Advocates for the use of various forms of technology identify increased access and opportunity, lower costs, improved coordination of services, and privacy for stigmatized individuals as benefits of the tools [8, 27, 37]. Critics, on the other hand, point to the technological difficulties that can impede interaction. They cite frustration with the technology, inequalities in access to the technology resources, confidentiality concerns, and depersonalization [17, 18, 26, 35]. These issues must be addressed when considering the use of e-health tools in social work.

Technological difficulties

Social workers traditionally consider themselves "people-centered". Their education revolves around understanding of human behavior in social environments and the development of relational and interaction skills. Social workers who choose to use technology as a tool for practice must understand how to "problem-solve" the inevitable technological problems that arise. As easy to use as the Internet may seem, it can be equally mystifying as interaction is suddenly halted because the connection is cut off, apparently without reason. Given the numerous types of hardware and software as well as modem connections and Internet Service Providers, understanding basic technological problem can be challenging. Although frustrating to an educated professional, it is even more so to a vulnerable client at the other end of the connection. Moreover, while the use of information technology is gaining in popularity, most social workers and clients have not had formal computer training. Social workers and clients need to be prepared with backup agreements for communication when their technological tools fail to respond and service is suddenly interrupted.

Inequality of access to technological resources

Although the cost of technology, especially that of desktop computers, is more affordable, the financial burden of not only hardware and software but also the Internet connection, is often a barrier for low income families [38]. Access to computer networks by poor underserved populations, makes the provision of service a difficult task in the "digital divide" [39]. And further, public access through institutions such as libraries and schools make the importance of privacy and confidentiality issues central to the technology controversy. Low income individuals sitting at a computer in a public library chatting online with their social worker or participating in their online support group are vulnerable to breaches of their privacy.

Confidentiality

Protection of client confidentiality is a central premise of the Social Work Code of Ethics [1]. Controversy exists over the ability to protect client data in a computer, especially the information shared over the Internet. Besides the difficulties preventing computer "hackers" from spying on therapists computer information, hidden files (text residue) left behind when files are seemingly deleted cause some concern [18]. Managing case notes and chat logs over web-based systems, and records of online conversations, can become burdensome given the security and privacy challenges of the medium.

On the positive side, some argue that the anonymity of the Internet actually protects confidentially and serves to improve access to service for those who may not access service otherwise. Individuals who are stigmatized, shy or embarrassed to share their problems are "faceless" over the world wide web and have been found to be more willing to participate in groups dealing with delicate issues [34]. In a study of patients suffering from anal fissures, Vernberg found that the Internet provided a way for 86% of the patients in the study to discuss experiences usually considered taboo [34].

Depersonalization

The Clinical Social Work Foundation has expressed caution and reservation regarding the use of the Internet for counseling. The concluding remarks of their official position paper on Internet therapy states:

> So much human suffering has been caused by disconnection-disconnection between Individuals, between through and feeling, between body and mind-and e-therapy offers yet another form. Clients seek our services in order to improve the quality of their lives, the quality of their relationships. Alienation from others and the self will not be healed through a virtual connection in cyberspace, a 'connection' that is fraught with risks and hazards for both clients and clinicians [40].

One of the central issues for social workers involves the inability to assess visual non-verbal behavior. Social Workers are trained to observe clients non-verbal clues as they interact, using these behaviors as an important component in overall assessment. The lack of face-to-face interaction impedes a social workers ability to obtain a full picture, limiting an important tool for assessment [41].

A further challenge becomes the issue of identity and deception in so-called virtual communities. Web-based tools allow for the formation of social entities consisting of people who are brought together because of a common factor such as a medical condition (i.e. support groups for diabetic patients) or functional limitation. Virtual communities increasingly make use of standard information tools to support collaborative activities and communication between clients and social workers. Identity plays a key role in such virtual communities. In traditional settings, knowing the identity of those with whom ones communicates is essential for understanding and evaluating an interaction [42]. However, in the virtual community, identity is ambiguous. Many of the basic cues about personality and social roles we have come to expect in the "real" world, are not available via the web [43]. This becomes a challenge for professionals who participate in such communities, and a point of criticism of the use of e-health tools in social work.

Keys to the Future Success of e-health tools in social work practice

Three keys will determine the ultimate success of the social work profession with resolution of the current controversy and implementation of e-health tools. First, the initial use of a new technology, and the continued use of any tool, should be accountable to the same standards of practice as traditional social work. This would include practice and program evaluation of all technological innovations introduced into any setting. Secondly, the social work profession must acknowledge the use of these technologies and hold practitioners accountable to appropriate practice standards through the revision of the NASW Code of Ethics. Finally, social work practitioners must be trained on the use on these emerging technologies and on their possible benefits to practice settings. If tools are developed that improve the quality of life for clients, it is the responsibility of the profession to educate itself on these tools and make them available to clients. Not only does this training require learning technical skills required for computer use, but also the development of conceptual models and theory frameworks to guide these new practices [10].

The mediating factor in these controversies must be research. Research is necessary to examine the effectiveness of all forms of technology. If technology is a worthy tool for social services practice, it must be demonstrated as effective to the profession and as having positive outcomes for those it is designed to help. Sowers and Ellis note the critical importance of research to the implementation of any technological intervention [7]. More research is needed to measure effectiveness; few studies on outcomes exist [20]. Simply adopting technology without extensive needs-assessment and evaluation of the innovation will not result in credibility or in effective social work practice.

Evaluation efforts should include both formative and summative evaluation. Formative evaluation will monitor the effects of an e-health tool in social work practice as it is being designed, implemented and employed. Such an approach can lead to an improvement or redesign of the tool based on the feedback provided by social workers and their clients. A summative evaluation that will assess the impact of an e-health tool after its implementation and utilization will lead to conclusions that can inform other e-health initiatives in social work. Some argue that a participatory evaluation is best indicated for interventions in social work [44]. Participatory evaluation aims to be practical in that it respond to the needs, interests and concerns of their primary users; useful because findings are disseminated in ways in which primary users can use them; and formative because they seek to improve program outcomes [45]. Thus, this approach seems to address the evaluation needs in the context of e-health employment in the social work field. Regardless of the approach and methodology, however, extensive evaluation and research studies are needed, as stated above, when introducing new technologies in a professional field.

Establishment of Practice Guidelines

The social work profession has been built on a standardized and well articulated Code of Ethics and set of core values [46]. These traditions do not directly speak to the issues unique to online service provision. This results in social workers using them without solid professional practice standards. One study conducted in 1997 found that most home pages offering online counseling provided little information about the qualifications of those providing the services [38]. Because licensing laws differ between regions, regional standards are not the answer as the virtual world breaks down geographic barriers and a social worker can be in one part of the country, treating a client not only in a different region, but in a different part of the world.

In the United States, the need for the National Association of Social Workers to revise professional standards and recognize the rising number of members using e-health tools is becoming urgent. Markson identified ideas for modification and interpretation of current practice standards in 2000 [47]. More specific practice standards were identified by Menon in 2002 [18]. These revisions included addressing issues of confidentiality, web security, transmission of information, development of standards regarding the types of clients to receive technological interventions, addressing issues of credentialing, and identifying hardware and software requirements to assure privacy and safety [18]. The revision of the NASW Code of Ethics or the development of an entirely new and separate set of standards for the profession of online services needs to be a priority for the organization traditionally recognized as maintaining the integrity of the social work profession.

Education of professionals

As Distance Education courses gain momentum in schools of social work and social workers become more familiar and comfortable with the use of technology for personal learning, the use of e-health tools will become increasingly popular. While research has shown that social work is taking technology into account, the inclusion of information technology (IT) principles into the curricula has been noted as problematic as it is done with out-of-date perspectives and information [48]. Grebel and Styaert researched the application of IT in schools of social work in 11 countries in Europe. They found that schools differed dramatically on the level of attention, integration into the curriculum, and the availability of technological tools and equipment. They conclude that the training and integration of information technology into the curriculum is not sufficient to meet the needs of the practice environment [48].

Schools of Social Work need to retool their faculty, students, and alumni with the skills required to practice in the information age. The future provision of social services requires practitioners to understand how to handle digital information, how and when to use various e-tools, how various types of clients can benefit from e-tools, and how to measure the effectiveness of a practice using e-tools for intervention. As social work education has embraced a generalist practice model, teaching general skills to practitioners regardless of the setting for the practice, so must it enhance teaching of "technical skills" regardless of the media for delivery. Group skills need to be learned not only for face-to-face interaction, but for online interaction within structured support group practices. Assessment skills not only of non-verbal behavior, but also the "expressive behavior" found online through the use of various symbols. The new skills, behaviors, and language of an Internet age need to be integrated into the traditional knowledge, skills, and science of the profession [49].

Conclusion

This chapter focused on the integration of e-health tools in social work and discussed the challenges and emerging trends. It becomes clear that new concepts and approaches are emerging in the field of social work. A study by Grebel and Steyaert in the Netherlands use a concept termed *social informatics* and provide a helpful context for social work educators. Social informatics is defined as "the ability to gather and interpret data efficiently and effectively into functional information for professional acting in social work settings, effectively making use of IT applications" (p. 162) [48]. Social informatics, developed in the Netherlands, advocates the infusion of IT into an existing curriculum, rather than the creation of a specific IT course [50]. This model challenges schools of social work to seriously address technology and training, validating its importance to practice and to the profession.The Netherlands model of Social Informatics creates an opportunity for the disciplines of Social Work and Informatics to collaborate in finding ways to implement e-health tools in human services. As Informatics' academicians and other IT technicians continue to develop e-health tools for human services, early collaboration with social work professionals will help assure product usability, and practicality. As social workers move these new e-health tools into practice settings, they can benefit from the technical expertise and experience of IT designers and researchers as tools are implemented into real world settings.

Collaborating with experienced IT professions, social workers will find innovative ways to improve care to underserved populations in a safe, cost effective manner demonstrating positive outcomes, under the guidance of accepted professional standards. This collaboration can address the current controversies of the profession through interdisciplinary problem solving and innovation combined with outcome based data collection. The future is promising.

References

[1] National Association of Social Workers, *Code of Ethics*, http://www.socialworkers.org/pubs/code/code.asp.

[2] Barker, R.L., *The social work dictionary*. 3rd ed. 1995, Washington, DC: NASW Press.

[3] Dziegielewski, S., *The Changing Face of Health Care Social Work*. Springer Series on Social Work, ed. A. Roberts. 1998, New York, NY: Springer Publishing.

[4] McCarty, D. and C. Clancy, *Telehealth: implications for social work practice*. Social Work, 2002. **47**(2): p. 153-61.

[5] Bashshur, R., *Telemedicine and the health care system*, in *Telemedicine: Theory and Practice*, R. Bashshur, J.H. Sanders, and G.W. Shannon, Editors. 1997, Charles C Thomas: Springfield, Ill.

[6] Richmond, M.E., *Social diagnosis*. 1911, New York: Russell Sage Foundation.

[7] Sowers, K. and R. Ellis, *Steering currents for the future of social work*. Research on Social Work Practice, 2001. 11(2): p. 245-253.

[8] Chenoweth, L., *Using technology in rural practice-local area coordination in rural Australia*. Rural Social Work, 2002. 7(1): p. 14-21.

[9] Robin, S.C., R. Reardon, and B.V. Strand, *A video streaming pilot project: Applications in social work training and education*. Journal of Technology in Human Services, 2001. 18(3/4): p. 133-143.

[10] Galinsky, M.J. and J.H. Schopler, *Connecting group members through telephone and computer groups*. Health and Social Work, 1997. 22(3): p. 181-189.

[11] Doolittle, G., *A cost measurement study for a home-based telehospice service*. J Telemed Telecare, 2000. 6(Supp 1): p. S193-S195.

[12] Pardeck, J.T., *Rationalizing decision-making through computer technology: a critical appraisal*. Journal of Health and Social Policy, 1998. 9(4): p. 19-29.

[13] Schoech, D., et al., *Developing and using a community databank*. Computers in Human Services, 1998. 15(1): p. 35-53.

[14] McCoy, V.H. and C.K. Vila, *Tech knowledge: Introducing computers for coordinated care*. Health and Social Work, 2002. 27(1): p. 71-74.

[15] Ouellette, P.M. and S. Sells, *Creating a telelearning community for training social work practitioners working with troubled youth and their families.* Journal of Technology in Human Services, 2001. 18(1/2): p. 101-116.

[16] Rosenfield, M., *Electronic technology for social work education and practice: The application of telephone technology to counseling.* Journal of Technology in Human Services, 2002. 20(1/2): p. 173-181.

[17] Schopler, J.H., M.D. Abell, and M.J. Galinsky, *Technology-based groups: A review and conceptual framework for practice.* Social Work, 1998. 43(3): p. 254-266.

[18] Menon, G.M. and J. Miller-Cribbs, *Online Social Work Practice: Issues and Guidelines for the Profession.* Advances in Social Work, 2002. 3(2): p. 104-116.

[19] Nartz, M. and D. Schoech, *Use of the Internet for community practice: A delphi study.* Journal of Community Practice, 2000. 8(1): p. 37-59.

[20] Meier, A., *Offering social support via the Internet: A case study for an online support group for social workers.* Journal of Technology in Human Services, 2000. 17(2/3): p. 237-266.

[21] Stocks, J.T. and P.P. Freddolino, *Evaluation of a World Wide Web-based graduate research methods course.* Computers in Human Services, 1998. 15(2/3): p. 51-69.

[22] Galambos, C. and C.E. Neal, *Macro practice and policy in cyberspace: teaching with computer simulation and the Internet at the Baccalaureate level.* Computers in Human Services, 1998. 15(2/3): p. 111-120.

[23] Seabury, B.A. and F.E. Maple, *Using computers to teach practice skills.* Social Work, 1993. 38(4): p. 430-439.

[24] Huff, M. and S. Edwards, *Using technological tools to enhance learning in Social Work diversity courses.* Journal of Technology in Human Services, 2001. 18(1/2): p. 51-64.

[25] McNutt, J., *Organizing cyberspace: strategies for teaching about community practice and technology.* Journal of Community Practice, 2000. 7(1): p. 95-109.

[26] Stofle, G.S. and S. Harrington, *Treating addictions on the Internet: Can it be done? A dialogue.* Journal of social work practice in the addictions, 2002. 2(2): p. 85-92.

[27] Giffords, E.D., *Social Work on the Internet: An Introduction.* Social Work, 1998. 43(3): p. 243-251.

[28] Demiris, G., et al., *Hospice attitudes toward "Tele-hospice".* American Journal of Hospice & Palliative Care, In Press.

[29] Taenzer, P.A., et al., *Computerized quality-of-life screening in an oncology clinic.* Cancer Practice, 1997. 5(3): p. 168-75.

[30] Skinner, H. and B. Allen, *Does the computer make a difference? Computerized versus face-to-face versus self-report assessment of alcohol, drug, and tobacco use.* J Consult Clin Psychol, 1983. 51: p. 267-275.

[31] Drummon, H., et al., *Electronic quality of life questionnaires: A comparison of pen-based electronic questionnaires with conventional paper in a gastrointestinal study.* Qual Life Res, 1995. 4: p. 21-26.

[32] Simpson, S., *Erasing the miles.* Assisted Living Today, 2001(April): p. 63-65.

[33] Cohen, L.J., *Phenomenology of therapeutic reading with implications for research and practice of bibliotherapy.* The Arts in Psychotherapy, 1994. 21: p. 37-44.

[34] Vernberg, D. and M.J. Schuh, *Internet Biolotherapy: A narrative anaysis of a reading simulated support group.* Journal of Social Work Disability and Rehabilitation, 2002. 1(1): p. 81-97.

[35] Kreuger, L. and J. Stretch, *What is the Role of Hypertechnology in Social Work Today?* Social Work, 2000. **45**(5): p. 457-462.

[36] Karger, H.J. and L. Kreuger, *Technology and the not always so human services*, in *Technology and Human Services*, J.W. Murphy and J.T. Pardeck, Editors. 1988, Haworth Press: New York. p. 111-126.

[37] Smart, J., J. Russell, and C. Custodio, *Developing a computerized health record in a protective services system.* Child Welfare, 1998. 77(3): p. 347-62.

[38] Sampson, J.P., R.W. Kolodinsky, and B.P. Greeno, *Counseling on the information highway: Future possibilities and potential problems.* Journal of Counseling and Development, 1997. 75(3): p. 203-212.

[39] Larrison, C., et al., *Welfare recipients and the digital divide: left out of the new economy?* J of Technology in Human Services, 2002. **19**(1): p. 1 12.

[40] Clinical Social Work Federation, *CSWF position paper on Internet text-based therapy.* 2001.

[41] Coleman, M., *Online therapy and the clinical social worker.* 2000, NASW Social Work Practice Update: Washington, DC.

[42] Saville-Troike, M., *The Ethnography of Communication.* 1982, London: Basil Blackwell.

[43] Donath, J., *Identity and Deeption in the Virtual Community*, in *Communities in Cyberspace*, M. Smith and P. Kollock, Editors. 1998, Routledge: London.

[44] Cousins, J.B. and L.M. Earl, *The case for participatory evaluation.* Educational Evaluation and Policy Analysis, 1992. 14: p. 397-418.

[45] Tandon, R., *Social transformation and participatory research.* Convergence, 1988. 21: p. 5-15.
[46] National Association of Social Workers, *NASW Code of Ethics*. 2004.
[47] Marson, S., M. and S.B. Brackin, *Ethical interaction in cyberspace for social work practice.* Advances in Social Work, 2000. 1(1): p. 27-41.
[48] Grebel, H. and J. Steyaert, *Social informatics: beyond technology A research project in schools of social work in the European Community.* International Social Work, 1995. 38: p. 151-164.
[49] Riva, G., *The sociocognitive psychology of computer-mediated communication: The present and future of technology-based interactions.* Cyberpsychology & Behavior, 2002. 5(6): p. 581-598.
[50] Roosenboom, P., *The Dutch National Curriculum Computer Applications for Schools of Social Work*, in *Technology in People Services, Research Theory and Applications*, C. Leiderman, et al., Editors. 1993, The Haworth Press: New York. p. 319-327.

Telework for Persons with Disabilities in the EU and the USA: What Can We Learn from Each Other?

Laura H. SCHOPP, Ph.D.
University of Missouri-Columbia, USA
Department of Health Psychology

Abstract. Persons with disabilities represent a growing population in both the European Union (EU) and the United States (USA). The ability to work is a key component in achieving independence and full inclusion in society, and employability is increasingly seen as an important outcome variable for studies in health and disability. However, persons with disabilities face considerable challenges in returning to work due to barriers related to transportation, job changes after disability, lack of support services in the workplace, and related barriers. Telework, or work from a distance, may help to mitigate these obstacles, while expanding the range of work options available for persons with disabilities. The EU has made substantial policy progress to support telework, but persons with disabilities have had only limited long-term success in telework initiatives due to lack of work support services. The USA has generally strong support services but lacks telework policy infrastructure. The EU and the USA can benefit from collaborative work to enhance their complementary strengths.

Key Terms: Telework, disability, vocational rehabilitation

This manuscript was produced with support from the National Institute on Disability & Rehabilitation Research (#H133G)20065 & #H133N000012-02), U.S. Department of Education. Opinions expressed here do not reflect the opinions of the Department of Education.

Introduction

2003 was the European Year of People With Disabilities, reflecting growing concern about the status of individuals with disabilities throughout the EU. Disability affects a large sector of the EU public, as one in six working-age persons in EU Member States has a disability that affects their work and functioning [1]. The number of Europeans who live with disabilities is also growing, due in large part to the aging population in industrialized countries.

With this growing rate of disability, it will be necessary to develop solutions that enable persons with disabilities to make productive work contributions to Member States, despite barriers to participating in the traditional workplace. Teleworking, or working from a distance, has received strong support from the European Commission, and is likely to offer one such solution. Telework is a priority of the European Commission because it has very favorable potential social implications, such as decreased pollution, increased worker flexibility, better collective use of networked employment resources that can be used by many companies or many workers, and reduced burdens related to transportation and commuting. Persons with disabilities are likely to benefit substantially from teleworking opportunities, as accessible transportation remains a significant barrier to work outside the home or neighborhood [2].

1. The E.U.'s Commitment to Teleworking and Disability Employment

Telework policy in the EU is relatively mature, even if its implementation lags somewhat behind such policy gains. In July 2002, EU-level social partner organizations entered into a formal framework agreement on telework. Signatories included EU-level organizations representing business, management, public and private sector enterprises, and trade unions. The document was seen as a watershed event because it secured definitions of teleworkers, data protection, liability, health and safety, and collective rights of teleworkers [3].

1.1 Telework Rates and Policy in the EU

Telework has enormous potential economic impact in the EU. However, estimates of the rate of teleworking are quite variable across EU Member States. A 1999 survey revealed that 17% of Finland's workforce reported that their primary or supplemental work involved some form of telecommuting or working from home, whereas Spain had the lowest rate of telework at 2% [4].

Telework may provide an excellent means by which Europeans with disabilities can demonstrate their capacity for independence and creative work contributions to the Information Society [5], and EU disability employment policy reflects this opportunity. The European Union's employment strategy for persons with disabilities is outlined in the 1999 Title on Employment in the Treaty of Amsterdam Employment Guidelines. Guideline 9 of this document directs Member States to use resources to develop preventive and *active* policies that will result in integration of persons with disabilities into the labor market [6]. Guideline 3 further stipulates that Member States will benefit from research to "identify good practice in the field of disability and anti-discrimination" [6], and that disability policy focus is shifting to the social and employment opportunities made possible by the advent of the Information Society. With respect to telework, Guideline 3 notes that the Information Society is "likely to be a more positive and inclusive environment for disabled people to live and work" [6].

1.2 Benefits and Barriers to U.S./E.U. Telework Cooperation

The nations of the European Union have led efforts to prioritize telework and to move telework from the concept stage to implementation [7]. In the 1980s and 1990s, the European Commission sponsored a number of pilot projects to test the feasibility of teleworking for persons with disabilities. For example, some pilot projects developed telecentres, in which workers used space in the nearest available centre and worked from that telecentre with colleagues networked across cities or across countries. Telecottages were a rural variant of the telecentre idea, in which the opportunity to work for predominantly urban-based high-tech companies is made available through networked rural office outposts accessible to rural workers. Telecottages have been successful among the general population, particularly in Scandinavia, Ireland, Wales, France, England, and Scotland [5].

Despite some islands of teleworking success, the impact of teleworking to date has been generally disappointing among Europeans with disabilities. Despite the comparatively well-developed EU-wide policy emphasis on teleworking, a number of teleworking barriers have been identified at the level of supports for the individual worker. These individual-level barriers include lack of adequate training for telework among persons with disabilities, insufficient support for training, lack of assistive technology consultation where appropriate, and lack of support and job counseling services for persons with disabilities. [8]. These weaknesses at the individual service delivery level have resulted in a large number of pilot projects failing to achieve sustainability after funding from the European Commission expired, as well as marginal employment rates and job retention rates among teleworkers with disabilities.

2. Status of Telework in the USA

In comparison to EU services, United States Vocational Rehabilitation services are relatively strong with respect to individualized job counseling and assistive technology training and equipment. However, telework in the United States has generally ignored the policy dimension and focused almost exclusively on a home-based independent contract agent model. In so doing, the U.S. vocational rehabilitation service structure has almost completely failed to address system and community-level telework supports such as telework policy, telecentres, telecottages, employer incentives to hire teleworkers with disabilities, and other similar policy solutions that are relatively more mature in the EU. Therefore, U.S. workers are at risk for social isolation, often lack job benefits associated with working for an employer, lack networking opportunities that come with being part of a larger business or organization, and are therefore left to fend for themselves with or without the skills to handle the challenges of private entrepreneurship.

3. The Future of EU/USA Collaboration in Telework for Persons with Disabilities

The USA and the EU would benefit from an exchange that would enable each to benefit from their complementary strengths on service and policy levels, respectively. To accomplish a fruitful interchange, it is necessary to embark on a long-term plan of exchange and cooperation between the EU and the USA so that telework for persons with disabilities can capitalize on the best of both systems.

3.1 International Collaboration Activities to Foster Telework

Telework cooperation across the Atlantic will not evolve on its own, and will take concerted effort on the part of business interests, persons with disabilities, disability specialists, and researchers. Activities needed to support such collaboration include the following:

- Dialog between the leaders of the European Commission-supported European Telework Development project and USA-based disability and vocational rehabilitation specialists. Such an exchange will allow USA policy planners to understand the status and trajectory of existing EU telework programs.
- Assessing successes and limitations of specific EU and USA telework projects. For example, the Telecom Italia project has conducted telework initiatives in telecommunications services for persons with disabilities, and may be a source of information on facilitators and barriers to program implementation.
- Examining the standard of care in vocational support services for persons with disabilities who work from home in the EU and the USA. Such an assessment should include enabling legislation, standard policy, local variations, and actual

service availability. For example, it is not enough to know that agency policy allows for computer training and assistive technologies, but rather it is important to assess the degree to which such services are actually available to persons with disabilities in a variety of urban and rural settings.

- Identifying the extent to which the EU Framework Agreement on Telework has been implemented among persons with disabilities. This assessment can be conducted in collaboration with policy makers, advocacy groups, and individual teleworkers with disabilities throughout the EU.
- Assessing the extent to which Member States have moved from policy to implementation, and the lessons learned from such efforts. For example, Italy has proposed the Telelavoro Telecommercio Telecooperazione Law for Telework, and implementation activities have begun through small but growing local and member state initiatives [9].
- Identifying the funding status of current EU and European Commission telework programs geared specifically toward persons with disabilities.
- Collecting data from EU and USA business and social service sectors about policy disincentives to working among persons with disabilities (e.g., lost pensions, lack of supportive incentives for business to hire teleworkers with disabilities, etc.).
- Collecting specific local data on the availability of job counseling and assistive technology services for teleworkers with disabilities throughout Member States and individual states in the USA.
- Identifying payment streams for assistive technology to support disabled teleworkers with disabilities.
- Interviewing teleworkers in their work environments (home, telecentre, and/or community work centers) to identify facilitators and barriers to telework.

3.2 Potential Outcomes of EU/USA Telework Collaboration

Favorable outcomes (e.g., increased availability of teleworking options for persons with disabilities, increased job retention of teleworkers, decreased reliance on public assistance funding among Europeans and USA citizens with disabilities, etc.) are expected to result from a beneficial bi-directional flow of information between the U.S. and the EU. First, Vocational Rehabilitation policy makers in the USA will benefit from an intensive examination of the more mature policy infrastructure that undergirds the EU's teleworking initiatives. At the same time, EU policy makers will benefit from receiving information about the range and funding structures of intensive individual-level services available to USA teleworkers with disabilities (e.g. job counseling services, assistive technology services). Such services can likely improve the marginal past success rate of teleworking programs among Europeans and Americans with disabilities.

References

[1] Eurostat (2003). One in six of the EU working-age population report disability. News Release 142/2003, 5 December, 2003.

[2] Mook, B. (2003). Working from home helps disabled. Detroit News, Friday, November 21, 2003.

[3] European Foundation for the Improvement of Living and Working Conditions (2002). Social partners sign teleworking accord. Available online at www.eiro.eurofound.ie/2002/07/feature/eu0207204f.html.

[4] ECATT (1999). Benchmarking Progress on Electronic Commerce and New Methods of Work. Report available online at http://www.etd.org.uk/faq/faq-numb.htm#ecatt.

[5] European Telework Online (2003). Telework and People with Disabilities. Available online at www.eto.org.uk/twork/disindex.htm.
[6] European Commission (1999). Employment and Social Affairs: The Employment Strategy. Available online at europa.eu.int/comm./employment_social/sco-prot/disable/employment_en.htm.
[7] Stephanidis, C. (1997). Disabled and Elderly People in the Information Society. European Consortium on Informatics and Mathematics: ECRIM News, No. 28, January, 1997.
[8] INCLUDE (2003). TWIN: Teleworking for the Impaired, Networked Centers Evaluation: Policy Recommendations for supporting teleworking for people with disabililities in the European Union. T1003/W3/1/d/CSELT/MM Project Number T1003. Available online at www.stakes.fi/include/twin.html.
[9] Young, M. (2003). A law for telework: Legislative proposal for the promotion of telework. Available from Telelavoro Telecommercio Telecooperazione at www.mc.ink.it/telalavoro/law.

E-Health: Current Status and Future Trends
G. Demiris (Ed.)
IOS Press, 2004

Evidence-Based Retrieval in E-Health

Timothy B. PATRICK, PhD, George DEMIRIS, PhD,
Lillian C. FOLK, BSBA.
Department of Health Management and Informatics, School of Medicine,
University of Missouri-Columbia, USA

Abstract. In this chapter we address the issue of standards for information retrieval to support decision making in e-health. Specifically, we consider the issue of evidence-based retrieval in the e-health domains of the consumer, healthcare practitioner, healthcare researcher, and genomics researcher. We present the results of a preliminary study to assess the current state of evidence-based retrieval in e-health. Within this study, we reviewed articles in e-health and telemedicine to determine the extent to which authors provide details of the information retrieval strategies used, as well as evidence of the effectiveness of those strategies. We also examined the extent to which the associated journals require authors of reviews to explicitly provide details of information retrieval strategies that they used, as well as reporting any evidence for the effectiveness of those strategies.

Introduction

A biomedical endeavor, whether professional or that of a layperson, whether focused on self-care, or patient care, or on the discovery of gene function, is *evidence-based* only to the extent that both its decision-making and its retrieval of information are evidence-based. The requirement of evidence-based *decision-making* is a requirement that decisions should utilize the best available scientific information relevant to the case at hand. However, in order to utilize that information, the decision maker must first obtain it. If faulty means are used to obtain the scientific information on which decisions are based, then the quality of those decisions may suffer. Thus, the requirement of evidence-based *information retrieval* is a requirement that the information used to support decisions be obtained using the best available information retrieval methods.

The overall, long term objective of our research program is to contribute to evidence-based information retrieval in biomedicine. In this article we present the case for this research in the special domain of *e-health*. We first examine the breadth of e-health as an evidence-based endeavor. We next make the case for the need to attend to evidence-based retrieval in e-health. Finally, we present the results of a preliminary study to assess the current state of evidence-based retrieval in e-health. We review articles in e-health and telemedicine for the extent to which authors provide details of the information retrieval strategies used, as well as evidence of the effectiveness of those strategies. We also examine the extent to which the associated journals require authors of reviews to explicitly provide details of information retrieval strategies that they used and/or to report any evidence for the effectiveness of those strategies.

1. Evidence-Based Health

1.1 Domains of Activity

The overall province of the evidence-based approach to health may be organized by domains of activity. **Figure 1** shows related domains of evidence-based health from a patient or consumer centric point of view. The activity of each of the nested spheres takes place in a larger context, and is perhaps dependent on that larger context. The activity with regard to health of consumers takes place (in at least some circumstances) in the context of their being cared for or being under the care of healthcare professionals. The work of healthcare professionals, on the other hand, is to some extent dependent upon or is informed by the work of healthcare researchers, and the work of healthcare researchers by that of genomic (and other) researchers.

1.2 Two Aspects of Evidence-Based Health

Each of these domains of evidence-based activity may be assigned two aspects. As shown in **Figure 1**, one aspect is "decision making". Whether he or she is a lay consumer, or a healthcare practitioner, or a researcher, the decision maker should base his or her decisions on the best available evidence. Of course, in order to base his or her decisions on the best available evidence, the decision maker must first obtain that evidence. Often that evidence will be available only as stored in some public or private repository. This may include bibliographic sources, such as Medline, or factual databases such a medical records database or a molecular sequence database. Thus, we are brought to a second aspect of these domains of evidence-based activity, "information retrieval". In order for the decision maker (whether lay consumer or professional) to base his or her decision on the best available evidence, he or she must access and use that evidence, and this will often (but not always) require him or her to retrieve that evidence from information or knowledge repositories.

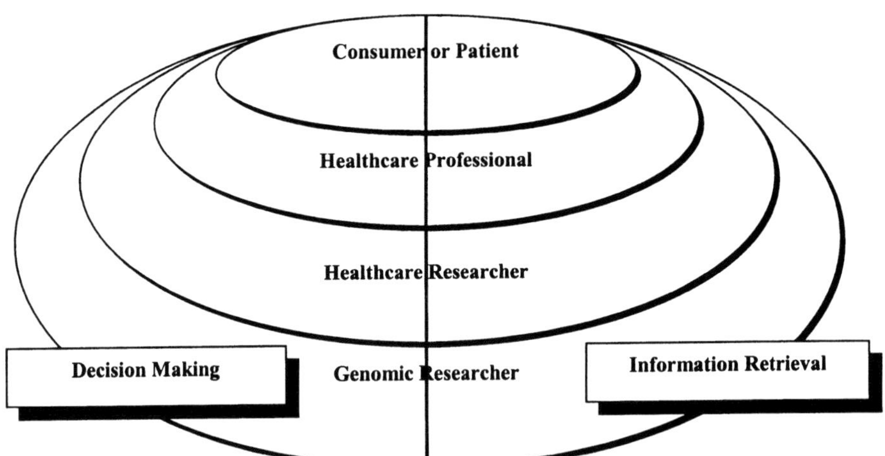

Figure 1. Two Aspects of Evidence-based Domains

2. Problems in Information Retrieval

2.1 Garbage In, Garbage Out
The phrase "garbage in, garbage out" is relevant to the overall process of retrieving evidence and then applying it in decision making in each of these evidence-based domains. In each domain, the information retrieval step may go badly awry, resulting in poor decisions and potential harm to patients.

2.2 Lay Consumer Domain
Information retrieval may certainly be a problem in the layperson domain. In particular, the quality of healthcare information available to laypersons (especially on the Internet) may be misleading or erroneous. [1] The availability of low-quality healthcare information poses a public health risk if consumers of that information tend to believe it and act on it. One study, for example, found that the free blood pressure monitors available to the public in retail stores in the U.S. are often miscalibrated, providing false and misleading information. Users of the monitors often believed them to be accurate and made health care decisions based on the readings. [2] Clearly, in that case the availability of low-quality information did appear to pose a health risk. We think it prudent to assume that the easy availability of false and misleading healthcare information on the Internet and other sources poses real health risks and should be taken seriously. We assume that there is a risk associated with information retrieval strategies chosen by laypersons, and to that extent laypersons should have good reasons for using the strategies they adopt.

2.3 Healthcare Professional Domain
Information retrieval may also be a problem in the healthcare professional domain. Indeed, proper methods of information retrieval are a major concern of "evidence-based medicine" training materials. For example the Centre for Evidence Based Medicine [3] includes a section entitled "Doing EBM" which discusses ways to formulate a good question, and how to search the literature to answer that question. These challenges of information retrieval need to be addressed during the medical curriculum and continuing medical education of health care providers who access information resources at the point of care in order to enhance the decision making process following the model of evidence-based clinical practice.

2.4 Healthcare Researcher Domain
Similarly, the effectiveness of methods of information retrieval is also an issue in the evidence-based domain of healthcare researchers. For instance, the recent death of a research volunteer participating in a study at Johns Hopkins was attributable to an inadequate information retrieval strategy used as a basis for the study. In its remarks on the case, the U.S. Department of Health and Human Services Office for Human Research Protection (OHRP) Compliance Determination Letter of 07/19/2001 specifically cited problems with the retrieval strategy used, saying

> "Prior to the research being approved by the IRB, the investigators and the JHBMC IRB failed to obtain published literature about the known association between hexamethonium and lung toxicity. Such data was readily available via routine MEDLINE and Internet database searches, as well as recent textbooks on pathology of the lung." [4]

Perhaps one of the more important sources of evidence in classical "evidence-based medicine" is the *meta-analysis*. Since information retrieval is an essential step in any meta-analysis, we would expect that retrieval to be well documented and its effectiveness well supported. Yet we recently conducted a study of a sample of published meta-analyses and found that in fact many of them did not report details of their retrieval strategy and most did not report any evidence of the effectiveness of their strategy. [5]

2.5 Genomic (and other) Researcher Domain

Finally, the effectiveness of methods of information retrieval may also be an issue in the domain of the genomic (or other *omic*) researcher. To take just one example, retrieval of information about the function of expressed genes in a microarray experiment is a complicated matter and one that is potentially fraught with difficulties. **Figure 2** depicts a possible flowchart for retrieval of gene function information using public resources from the National Center for Biotechnology Information (NCBI). As shown in the flowchart, there are various information sources available and there are conditional paths through the information space.

We investigated the state of evidence-based retrieval of gene function information in reports of microarray experiments. [6] This study found that many such reports do not indicate the retrieval methods used, and none of the studies we examined reported any evidence of the effectiveness of the retrieval strategy used.

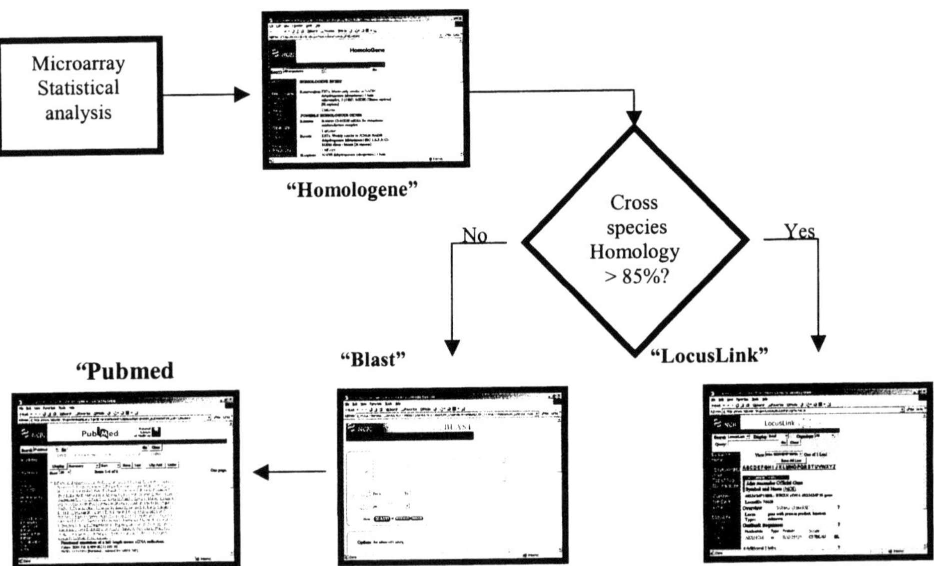

Figure 2. Possible Flowchart for Retrieval of Gene Function Information

3. *Evidence-Based* E-Health

We propose the following modification of the definition of e-health provided in the Introduction of this book:

> "*evidence-based* e-Health is defined as the use of advanced telecommunications such as the Internet, portable and other sophisticated devices, advanced networks and new design approaches aiming to support *evidence-based* healthcare delivery and education. Thus, *evidence-based* e-health refers to a fundamental redesign of healthcare processes based on the *evidence-based* use and integration of electronic communication at all levels."

Each of the domains of evidence-based health that we have considered has an "e-health" component, from consumer e-health to genomic (or other *omic*) e-science. Our position is that as each of these e-health domains is highly dependent on retrieval of digital information from on-line sources, they should be guided by evidence-based standards for information retrieval from those sources. To put the point bluntly, <u>if any domain of evidence-based health should pay attention to standards for evidence-based retrieval, e-health should.</u>

4. The Current State of Evidence-Based Retrieval in E-Health: A Preliminary Study

We carried out a preliminary study of the current state of evidence-based retrieval in e-health. The study consisted of two steps. In step 1 we examined review articles in e-health and telemedicine to investigate the extent to which authors provided details of the retrieval strategies used, as well as evidence of their effectiveness. In step 2 we examined the editorial policies of the journals in which those review articles were published, at least insofar as those editorial policies are represented by their "instructions to authors". Specifically, we were interested in the extent to which those journals require authors of reviews to explicitly provide details of information retrieval strategies that they used and/or to report any evidence for the effectiveness of those strategies.

4.1 Step 1: Analysis of Review Articles in e-health

4.1.1 Methods

We searched OVID [7] Medline subset 1966-January 2004 as follows:

1. TELEMEDICINE/
2. e-health.mp. [mp=title, abstract, name of substance, mesh subject heading]
3. 1 or 2
4. limit 3 to (human and english language and review articles)
5. limit 3 to (human and english language and systematic reviews)
6. 4 or 5

This search retrieved 350 citations. For this preliminary study, we limited the sample to those articles available in full text. This resulted in a study set of 43 articles covering 24 journals. Nine of those journals are included as core clinical journals of the Abridged Index Medicus (AIM). [8] The list of journals covered and their status is shown in **Table 1**.

Table 1. Journals Covered by the Full-text Sample

Journal	Abridged Index Medicus Core clinical Journal
AACN Clinical Issues	no
AJN, American Journal of Nursing	yes
Annals of Internal Medicine	yes
Annual Review of Public Health	no
Archives of Dermatology	yes
Archives of Ophthalmology	yes
Archives of Surgery	yes
BMC Medical Information & Decision Making	no
BMJ	yes
British Journal of Psychiatry	no
British Journal of Surgery	yes
Chest	yes
Clinical Obstetrics & Gynecology	no
CMAJ Canadian Medical Association Journal	yes
Current Opinion in Pediatrics	no
Journal of Nuclear Medicine Technology	no
Journal of Nuclear Medicine	no
Muscle & Nerve	no
Nursing & Health Care Perspectives	no
Nursing Standard	no
Pediatric Cardiology	no
Surgical Endoscopy	no
Telemedicine Journal & E-Health	no
World Journal of Surgery	no

We first classified each of the 43 articles as *relevant* or *irrelevant*. An article was *relevant* if it satisfied all of the following three conditions:

1. it was a review
2. it was focused on a single coherent theme or themes
3. it discussed e-health outcomes or made recommendations for e-health practice.

We next classified each of the relevant articles as describing or not describing a reproducible retrieval strategy. Finally we classified each article as providing or not providing evidence of the effectiveness of the reported strategy.

4.1.2 Results

Twenty articles out of the 43 were classified as relevant. Of these, only seven described a reproducible search strategy. None of these articles provided evidence of the effectiveness of its reported search strategy.

4.2 Step 2: Review of editorial policies of the journals

4.2.1 Methods

In Step 2 of our preliminary study we visited the web sites of the journals of articles classified as relevant and examined the instructions to authors provided there. We first classified these journals according to whether they included some instruction, either directly or via a reference to the Uniform Requirements for Manuscripts Submitted to Biomedical Journals (ICMJE) [9], the Quality of Reporting of Meta-Analyses (QUOROM) statement [10], or the Meta-Analysis Of Observational Studies in Epidemiology (MOOSE) statement [11] to provide details for a reproducible search. The ICMJE instructs authors to

> [i]dentify the methods, apparatus (give the manufacturer's name and address in parentheses), and procedures in sufficient detail to allow other workers to reproduce the results.

The QUOROM statement instructs authors to provide a description of their search strategy

> ...in detail (e.g., databases, registers, personal files, expert informants, agencies, hand-searching), and any restrictions (years considered, publication status, language of publication).

The MOOSE statement instructs authors to describe:

> Qualifications of searchers (e.g., librarians and investigators)
> Search strategy, including time period included in the synthesis and keywords.
> Databases and registries searched
> Search software used, name and version, including special features used (e.g., explosion)

Since the MOOSE statement requires authors to describe the qualifications of the searchers, it does at least to that extent require authors to provide evidence of the effectiveness of the information retrieval strategy used. We also classified the journals of relevant articles as to whether they included some instruction, either directly or via a reference to MOOSE, that authors provide some evidence of the effectiveness of the search strategy used.

4.2.2 Results

Thirteen of the 24 journals were associated with articles classified as relevant. **Table 2** shows the thirteen journals associated with relevant articles. Of these thirteen, three journals were excluded from further analysis because they did not provide instructions to authors.

The "instructions to authors" of four of the remaining 10 journals included no instruction, either directly or via a reference to ICMJE, QUOROM, or MOOSE, to provide details for a reproducible search. Only one of the six journals requiring search details also included a requirement, through a reference to MOOSE, that authors provide some evidence of the effectiveness of the search strategy used.

Table 2. Thirteen Journals Associated with Relevant Articles

Journal	Instructions to Authors Available	Requires Details of a Reproducible Search	Requires Evidence of the Effectiveness of Strategy
BMC Medical Information & Decision Making	yes	QUOROM,	MOOSE
BMJ	yes	QUOROM	no
British Journal of Surgery	yes	ICMJE; QUOROM	no
CMAJ Canadian Medical Association Journal	yes	ICMJE	no
Current Opinion in Pediatrics	yes	no	no
Journal of Nuclear Medicine	yes	ICMJE	no
Nursing Standard	yes	no	no
Pediatric Cardiology	yes	no	no
Surgical Endoscopy	yes	no	no
Telemedicine Journal & E-Health	yes	ICMJE	no
AACN Clinical Issues	no	NA	NA
Annual Review of Public Health	no	NA	NA
Clinical Obstetrics & Gynecology	no	NA	NA

4.3 Limitations of the Preliminary Study

We searched on OVID using a Boolean disjunction of the check boxes "review" and "systematic review". That strategy actually provided us with a number of articles that were not rigorous reviews of e-health or telemedicine. A further limitation was the restriction to articles available in full text. That restriction, though included for practical reasons in this preliminary study, may have skewed our results.

5. Conclusion

Many argue that the practice of e-health will revolutionize the health care field and redesign the process of care delivery by empowering patients and redefining the patient-provider relationship. We have argued that for any evidence-based endeavor, not only must its decision making be evidence-based, but its methods for retrieving that evidence should also be evidence-based. We have also argued that if any domain of evidence-based health should pay attention to standards for evidence-based retrieval, e-health should. Yet our preliminary results indicate that the science and practice of e-health includes reviews of the literature that do not report their retrieval strategies in sufficient detail to be repeated, or do not report evidence of the effectiveness of those strategies. The e-health revolution, for all its promise, must evolve further to its potential as evidence-based science and practice, and demand of its practitioners an adherence to improved standards of evidence-based retrieval.

References

[1] Impicciatore P, Pandolfini C, Casella N, Bonati M. Reliability of health information for the public on the World Wide Web: systematic survey of advice on managing fever in children at home. Bmj 1997;314(7098):1875-9.

[2] Thiedke CC, Laird S, Detar T, Mainous A, Jenkins K, Ye X. Patient Use of Automatic Blood Pressure Measures in Retail Stores: Implications for Diagnosis and treatment of Hypertension. Journal of the SC Medical Association 98(2):62-66.

[3] Centre for Evidence based medicine [URL: http://www.cebm.net/searching.asp]

[4] U.S. Department of Health and Human Services Office for Human Research Protection (OHRP) Compliance Determination Letter of 07/19/2001 [URL: http://ohrp.osophs.dhhs.gov/detrm_letrs/jul01a.pdf]

[5] Patrick TB, Demiris G, Folk LC, Moxley DE, Mitchell JA, Tao D. Evidence-Based Retrieval in Evidence-Based Medicine. J Med Libr Assoc 92(2):106-109.

[6] Folk LC, Patrick TB, Demiris G. Evidence-Based Retrieval for Discovery of Gene Function. Medinfo 2004, abstract, in press.

[7] OVID, [URL: http://www.ovid.com].

[8] Abridged Index Medicus (AIM) Journal Titles, National Library of Medicine [URL: http://www.nlm.nih.gov/bsd/aim.html]

[9] Uniform Requirements for Manuscripts Submitted to Biomedical Journals. International Committee of Medical Journal Editors.[Erratum Appears in JAMA 1998 Feb 18;279(7):510]. JAMA. 1997;277(11):927-34.

[10] Moher, D., Cook, D. J., Eastwood, S., Olkin, I., Rennie, D., and Stroup, D. F. Improving the Quality of Reports of Meta-Analyses of Randomised Controlled Trials: the QUOROM Statement. Quality of Reporting of Meta-Analyses. Lancet. 11-27-1999;354(9193):1896-900.

[11] Stroup, D. F., Berlin, J. A., Morton, S. C., Olkin, I., Williamson, G. D., Rennie, D., Moher, D., Becker, B. J., Sipe, T. A., and Thacker, S. B. Meta-Analysis of Observational Studies in Epidemiology: a Proposal for Reporting. Meta-Analysis Of Observational Studies in Epidemiology (MOOSE) Group. JAMA. 2000;283(15):2008-12.

The Impact of Genomics on E-Health

Joyce A. MITCHELL, PhD
University of Missouri-Columbia
Columbia, MO USA 65211

Abstract. The Human Genome Project (HGP) and e-Health are two fundamental changes that will alter the way we approach human health and life. These two scientific and societal forces will inevitably impact each other. This paper not only explores the ways that the HGP will change health care but also investigates the ways that e-Health systems will be influenced by the genomic data. The Electronic Medical Record (EMR) is discussed at length, including the probable impact on the laboratory, pharmacy, computerized provider order entry (CPOE), and other components. Thirteen points of a possible genomic future involving the EMR are presented. The genomic impact on other e-Health systems includes those at all levels of data: population, disease, patient, tissue and organ banks, cellular and for specific genes. The genomic impact on consumer health systems is explored, including Internet consumer information resources and the movement for direct-to-consumer genetic testing. The paper concludes that technology and trends of e-Health will enable the upcoming revolution caused by the health implications of the research emanating from the Human Genome Project.

1. Introduction

The Human Genome Project and e-Health each have great potential to fundamentally change the way we approach human health and threats thereto. Together they represent a tremendous opportunity/force for synergistic change and the improvement in the quality of life.

The Human Genome Project (HGP) has been an international research effort to determine the nucleotide sequences of all of the twenty-three pairs of chromosomes in human beings and the genomes of selected model organisms. This project began in 1990 and was completed in 2003, two years ahead of schedule [1]. Approximately 35,000 genes have been charted within the human DNA sequences. Today's research has turned from determining the sequences to the more difficult tasks of determining the function and regulation of the genes, the significance of variations among people and the potential for "genomic health care" including therapies, cures, and individualized medicine [detailed at the National Human Genome Research Institute (NHGRI) [http://www.nhgri.nih.gov/]. The HGP has already been the catalyst for changing biological sciences into an information science [2,3]. The HGP also holds the larger promise of transforming the way health care is practiced so that each individual is given personalized advice and treatment based on his/her genome [4].

E-Health has already been defined in the introduction to this book. E-Health involves the use of advanced telecommunications to support health care delivery and education, and will involve a fundamental redesign of health care processes to be fully realized. E-Health has been on the health care scene since the 1960's when computers were adopted for business systems and departmental clinical systems. However, within the past ten years e-Health has gained momentum from the rapid development of technologies used outside of the health care arena such as the Internet, the personal computer, PDAs, and cell phones. E-Health is developing rapidly with the application of these technologies to the health domain in such uses as consumer health, telemedicine, nanotechnologies, electronic medical records, health-care quality systems, and, with the spur of various government regulations such as HIPAA.

Two such fundamental changes happening to health care simultaneously will inevitably impact each other. This paper not only explores the ways that the HGP will change health care but also investigates the ways that e-Health systems will be influenced by the genomic data. The conclusion is that the trends in e-Health will enable the upcoming revolution caused by the health implications of the genome projects.

2. Impact of Genomics on Health Care

Physicians have known since the early 1900's that mutations in genes were the cause of specific diseases. Alkaptonuria, an inborn error of metabolism, was the first disease postulated to be inherited in an autosomal recessive pattern by Sir Archibald Garrod in 1902 [5]. Years later it was found that alkaptonuria was caused by a loss of homogentisate 1,2 dioxygenase function, and it wasn't until 1997 that the gene was cloned and sequenced [6]. Since the inception of the HGP, knowledge of the DNA sequences of specific genes and their molecular function has been growing rapidly. Within the past two years, the number of genes linked to specific health conditions has grown from approximately 1275 to 1600[1], an increase of 325. Whereas this represents less than 5% of the 35,000 genes of the human genome, it is a large enough set of specific knowledge that it is changing the health care landscape and challenging many health care providers. Slightly over 1000 of these 1600 genes are available for specific genetic tests through routine physician orders [7]. A list of all available genetic tests offered by laboratories worldwide can be found online at http://www.genetests.org.

Examples where the nature of the disease has been determined and its treatment or management has changed accordingly are illustrated by these six categories of genomic medicine:

(1) Ataxia-telangiectasia is caused by a single change in an amino acid in the ATM gene in both chromosomes of the person. In this case, the physician taking care of such a person would not only discuss the risks of the condition and its health care implications and risks to the child, but also the risks to other family members throughout their lives. The risks to other family members include the fact that carriers of the gene mutation are at an increased risk of multiple types of cancers, because the ATM gene is a DNA repair enzyme,

(2) A second example would be from more or less genetic material than most people. Huntington's Chorea is caused by a type of mutation called a "repeat expansion" where a small set of three nucleotides is repeated an unusually large number of times; the number of repeats is correlated with the age of onset of the disease. The physician would need to discuss testing of other family members and appropriate planning for assistance in later life.

(3) A third type of example comes from a genetic change that determines the ability (or inability) of a person to metabolize a drug in the same manner as the majority of the populace. Certain changes in cytochrome P450 genes cause a person to metabolize drugs more slowly or more rapidly than most people. The CYP2D6 gene (a member of the CYP450 gene family) has been shown to result in either exaggerated drug effects (e.g. tricyclic antidepressants) or diminished drug effect (e.g. codeine) or even ulta-rapid

[1] Derived from a search over time (January 2002 to February 2004) of the LocusLink database http://www.ncbi.nlm.nih.gov/locuslink with the specific query for organism=human and disease_known AND has_seq.

metabolism in some drugs [8]. This depends on whether the CYP2D6 gene is involved in the inactivation pathway or the activation pathway of a drug and which allele is present. The physician would need to be wary of prescriptions for medications that involve the cytochrome oxidative pathways and adjust dosages accordingly.

If a person has the A1555G mutation in a specific mitochondrial gene, this person is susceptible to hearing loss if he/she takes aminoglycosides [9,10]. The physician would need to avoid prescribing these medications altogether and to test other family members so that individuals carrying the gene would avoid the catastrophe of sudden and permanent hearing loss. Mitochondrial genes are inherited maternally, involving some specific genetic counseling that differs from standard Mendelian inheritance.

(4) A fourth type of change is where a genetic change causes the person to be more or less susceptible to an environmental agent. A classic example would be the carriers of mutations in the hemoglobin beta gene that confer a resistance to infection by the malaria virus, while people homozygous for the mutation are subject to a disease called sickle cell anemia. The physician becomes both a genetic counselor for future risks and also an advocate for the patient in pursuing (or not) certain employment opportunities or lifestyle choices.

(5) A fifth type of impact comes from the interaction with the person's nutrition and his/her genotype. The classic example would be phenylketonuria, an anchor of newborn screening programs. Individuals with PKU must alter their diet to avoid phenylalanine, an essential component of most sources of protein, because they cannot properly metabolize it. With the altered diet, individuals can avoid mental retardation and live productive lives. The physician must assist the person in monitoring his/her diet throughout his/her lifetime and especially during crucial reproductive periods.

(6) A sixth type of impact is emerging as specific medications are developed especially to treat those with predispositions to disease. An example is a fairly new cardiac disease marker, Lp-PLA2, that can be detected by the PLAC test [11]. Recently GSK (GlaxoSmithKline pharmaceuticals) has developed a drug that is targeted specifically to those individuals who test positive for the PLAC test and purported to decrease their risk of cardiac disease.

These six types of changes in health care are only illustrative of the nature of the knowledge and practice revolution that is steadily growing.

The health implications of the research emerging from the sequences determined by the Human Genome Project will be profound. Health implications stemming from the knowledge of the variations among specific individuals will cause patient-provider discussions to center increasingly on risks related to specific medications, nutrition, and environmental hazards [12,13,14]. Table 1 lists areas where health care is likely to change based on the emerging knowledge.

The implications for physicians will likely include these multiple aspects. Genetics is invading the mainstream of medical practice and will no longer be limited to subspecialty medicine [7]. Molecular diagnostics, the province of genetic testing, will revolutionize portions of the practice of pathology. Predictive diagnostic testing will be increasingly practiced as part of primary care medicine. This will make discussions of risk commonplace, and will often entail discussion of risks in cases where the patient is not ill. The major therapy recommendations for most patients will be behavior modification involving specific occupations, nutrition, medications, and lifestyle choices. Gene therapy, while important for some selected conditions, will come more slowly than the knowledge about behavior. Specific genetic tests will increasingly be required before medications can be prescribed.

The health care system as a whole will also experience significant impacts. The insurance industry (especially in the United States) will be pressed by impending legislation mandating non-discrimination for genetic conditions and genetic test results. When these non-discrimination laws are passed, the floodgates will open for more genetic tests. The FDA is poised to regulate the genetic testing panels likely to emerge for specific sets of conditions [14,15,16], the first of which will be drug metabolism panels and single gene conditions related to common disorders of adults. The current trend of direct-to-consumer orders of genetic tests will also likely expand. [17,18] The resulting health insurance industry will need to redefine the way it reimburses since personalized health care will demand specific recommendations depending on the constellation of genetic susceptibilities in each person.

Environmental risk factors will dictate OSHA-type approaches to worker empowerment and education about safe behavior [19]. Research in this area is burgeoning since the completion of the human genome sequence, including a registry to relate gene variants to environmental diseases [20]. This will necessitate much teamwork among workers and employers in order to avoid charges of discrimination.

Inevitably, there will be a continued gap between public perceptions of genetic research and the reality of the research. Furthermore, there will be a persistent fear of the unintended consequences of genetic research because it will continue to involve such politically and ethically charged issues as abortion, cloning, gene therapy, and stem cells. Manpower issues related to the need for genetic counselors will balloon, stemming from the need for all persons to discuss the implications for test results and resultant decisions.

Table 1. Health Implications of the Human Genome Project Research

Traditional Health care	**Genomics Health care – Personalized Medicine**
Single gene disorders were seen by specialists in genetics or sub-specialists in health care fields	Single genes are implicated in all common disorders. People with single gene disorders are seen by primary care providers.
Only a handful of genes were linked to specific health conditions	1600 genes have been linked to specific health conditions. The number is growing steadily and with implications for specific health care discussions. Direct-to-consumer testing is available.
A few rare conditions were linked to unusual drug metabolism. The anesthesiologist needed to know about these.	Many variants in genes are discovered that alter the rate of drug metabolism. All patients will have personalized dosage and drug regimes in the future.
A few genes were known to confer susceptibility to environmental factors.	Each person will have a list of genetic variants amenable to environmental manipulation. Behavioral modification will be the subject of patient-provider discussions.
Individuals with a few rare genetic conditions known to be influenced by nutrition were taken care of by specialists in inborn errors.	Each person will have a list of genetic variants (same as above) but to include specific dietary supplements and foods to avoid.

3. Impact of Genomics on e-Health Systems

All systems in the e-Health domain will feel the impact of the genomics revolution. The electronic medical record is already beginning to feel the effects; other systems are also affected, including those of all levels of health care as well internet-based health sites that are instrumental in the consumer health movement.

3.1 Impact on the Electronic Medical Record

The first issue to tackle within the electronic medical record (EMR) is what part of the genomic records to store and where to store them. The second issue is how to use these records for alerts, reminders, and patient safety.

A specific example will help to illustrate the points made here. A genetic test can be ordered to determine if a person had ataxia-telangiectasia; the ordering physician can decide to send a DNA specimen to a reference laboratory for a full genetic sequence determination. The results would be reported back not with the actual sequence but with a list of the variations from the "reference" sequence [21]. For many genes, this reference sequence is determined by the National Center for Biotechnology Information (NCBI) and is used world-wide; for the ATM (Ataxia Telangiectasia Mutated) gene it would be reference sequence NM 000051 for the DNA sequence and NP 000042 for the protein sequence for transcript variant 1 of the gene (the protein is currently known to have three isoforms). The cause of the disease would be listed as a change in the amino acid sequence of the protein (e.g. glu126asp), but the other polymorphisms recognized would be listed as a change in the nucleotide sequence of the DNA (e.g., CG at 126; most frequent genotype GG). The question at hand is how these test results would become part of the person's EMR.

It is highly unlikely that the entire genome of large numbers of individuals will be stored in the EMR for some time; this is because the cost of whole genome sequencing is prohibitive at present. The goal to sequence the genome of any individual for $1000 is probably 10-15 years in the future [22]. However, sequencing of single genes is routine in specialized gene testing laboratories such as the laboratory that performed the ATM test in the example. A significant impact of storing the results of the ATM DNA test would be that the result would be tied to an external reference source; this external reference is without precedence in the building of EMRs. This will mean that the EMR is hot-linked to a public reference database, further causing a dilemma when the external reference changes such as happens when more isoforms or polymorphisms or disease-causing mutations are discovered. The use of an external reference to an integral part of the EMR will likely not be the standard configuration in the short term; it is likely that many institutions would prefer to store the results of the test locally (probably as a scanned report) so that it is fully contained within the EMR until the nuances of the external reference links are determined. However, the use of an external reference may turn out to be the standard in the long run.

The sequence of single genes will likely become part of in-house EMRs within the next few years. Specific panels of gene tests are also being developed and will likely become part of the EMR in the immediate future. These panels will likely look for a set of variants or mutations known to cause disease instead of being a set of whole gene sequences. For example, a set of cytochrome oxidase gene variants is already commercially available to test for these enzymes that cause differences in drug metabolism among people; even consumers can send a blood sample to get the test panel [http://www.healthanddna.com/drugreactiontest.html]. This is similar to the panel of tests that constitute a newborn screen; a report on the results of the panel is stored as a text document within the EMR. As these tests become less expensive, it will be likely that the tests will include the full sequence of the genes included in the test panel.

It is unlikely that a DNA or protein sequence will be stored in any of the existing components of the EMR. It is more probable that gene sequence data will be stored in a separate component of the EMR that is yet to be developed. This data will not likely be accessed routinely by the users of the EMR but would more likely be accessed by computer programs that would search the data to match newly discovered disease patterns; this is because the data would consist largely of strings of DNA nucleotides or proteins along with location codes as to where this snippet of DNA arose on the chromosomes and the specific start point of the sequence. The ideal situation would be to determine the genetic sequence once and to keep it part of the health record of the individual for life, referring to it whenever needed without needing to determine the sequence a second time.

3.1.1 Impact on the Laboratory System

The laboratory systems that are interfaced to an EMR do not currently have the capacity to store the raw DNA or protein sequence but would presumably be the system that would store the results of genetic tests. These results would need to be augmented from a simple positive or negative test result in order to hold the metadata about the genetic test results. This would include the type of genetic test performed (i.e. full sequence versus mutant panel) and the specific result found (val3leu in the ATM gene). This meta-data would be augmented by a knowledge base to reference the implications of this test result (mutant phenotype causing a specific disease, a disease susceptibility mutation, polymorphism, etc). This component might be another example of a hot-link to an external reference source since it is difficult for the health system to keep up with all known variants and the health implications. These systems would likely be derived from candidates such as OMIM™ (Online Mendelian Inheritance in Man; http://www.ncbi.nlm.nih.gov/omim/), Human Genetic Mutation Database (HGMD®; http://archive.uwcm.ac.uk/uwcm/mg/hgmd0.html), and the Single Nucleotide Polymorphism database (dbSNP; http://www.ncbi.nlm.nih.gov/SNP). The molecular diagnostic laboratory subsystem would likely be the place where such specific tests results and reference links would be stored.

3.1.2 Impact on the Pharmacy System

The pharmacy system would be augmented by knowledge bases regarding the effect of genotypes likely to metabolize or transport specific drugs in a manner different from the average. Over thirty families of drug metabolizing and transporting enzymes have been found in humans [8]; the sheer number of variations among people makes this data very complicated. These data are already being maintained, but they are rapidly expanding and require frequent updating because of the accelerating pace of discovery. Currently, many clinical trials [see http://clinicaltrials.gov/ for federally and privately supported clinical trials] are being conducted on individuals who have specific genetic drug-metabolism variants. The pharmacy system would need to have an extensive alert system to warn providers about known variations of drug metabolism or toxic reactions to drugs. The current pharmacy systems use the EMR list of allergies to guard against adverse reactions; the future pharmacy systems will need to access a new module that includes drug susceptibilities.

3.1.3 Impact on Computerized Provider Order-Entry (CPOE)

The computerized provider order-entry system (CPOE) would be used for a set of alerts and reminders and as a system to safeguard patient safety. Several scenarios would trigger the alerts. First, a search for the patient's specific laboratory metadata would determine if the person had a known variant of the metabolism of the specific medication ordered. Second, in some circumstances the health system would determine that a medication could not be ordered unless a specific genetic test was first performed. An example of this would be testing of the A1555G mutation when placing an order for aminoglycosides in order to avoid antibiotic-induced deafness. The health system would need a team of professionals working to keep the system of alerts up-to-date and complete. Professional associations that focus on sets of genes or sets of diseases would augment this component. Other scenarios would trigger the patient reminders related to specific risks. The specific nature of the set of recommendations for an individual would work best if reminders were sent (by email or postcard) on a schedule determined by the physician to be optimal for the individual. A given patient might need to be followed more closely than standard for specific types of cancer or for complications of a chronic disease. This could be accommodated by an electronic reminder system tailored to the individual and based on an EMR component for "health risks and follow-up."

3.1.4 Impact on the EMR Globally

The general impact on the EMR from genomics data would be the need for several components that are part of most EMRs today but would need to be augmented to be able to respond fully to the challenges. The first of these is the reminder system mentioned above. The second component would be a part of the problem-based record that would concentrate on individual risks associated with the person's genotype and the preventive measures being developed. These "problems" would not always be immediate health concerns but would represent future possibilities. The risk profiles would be linked to the reminder systems in a set of clinical guidelines developed for these circumstances. The third would be to have a mechanism to search across all health records of the health system to determine which individuals are at risk for new disease associations determined by genomic research. Intelligent computer agents would likely perform this search on the genome component of the record. The fourth would be an enhanced EMR component to expand "known allergies" to include "genetic drug susceptibilities." Obviously regulations and privacy would be a prime concern for all parties.

Primary care providers cannot be expected to remember all information about all of the health implications of the specific genetic variants carried by their patients. Thus the incorporation of the Internet web sites is an essential component of the future of genomic medicine. The National Library of Medicine has recently teamed up with the American Academy of Physicians – American Society of Internal Medicine Foundation to promote a "Health Information Prescription" [23]. They are specifically recommending that the physician write a prescription for the patients to use MedlinePLUS (http://medlineplus.gov) when they have questions about the health conditions listed on that site. This site is linked to a consumer health site concentrating on the health implications of the HGP: the Genetics Home Reference (http://ghr.nlm.nih.gov) [24]. However, specific components of the person's genome records will likely be tied to Internet sites. These include the reference sequences for the DNA and proteins as well as the health implications of specific variations in the sequence. The latter is used in both the pharmacy system when it reports specific variants that have variant drug reactions and the laboratory system when it reports the significance of the genetic tests. This could include components similar to those of Gene Tests (http://www.genetests.org/) and Pharm GKB (http://pharmgkb.org).

3.1.5 Future Scenario of the Genome and EMR

The most likely future scenario (see table 2) for the whole genome sequence is that it will be routinely generated at birth as part of the future newborn screening system. The UK is preparing a pilot project to investigate this further [25]. Large scale systems will be required to determine the full genetic sequence with high accuracy and at a low cost. This sequence could be stored by each state for all people born in that state, but "owned" by the individual. The state system would be the steward of the genome. The data structure, format and accession rules would be governed by (inter)national standards. The sequence data would be secured against invasion by various computer mechanisms but would be available to those health systems with whom the individual was involved. The parents of a newborn would receive a printout with the risks and probabilities of various health conditions shortly after birth. The parents would not only discuss this with their child's pediatrician but could also discuss the report with entrepreneurial businesses whose specialty is the counseling of individuals about their genetic risks and future. The genetic risk profile would be updated periodically, based on the analysis of intelligent search programs that would incorporate information about the health implications of the genome project with specific DNA searching algorithms.

This scenario paints a rosy vision of the future. Full genome data would be stored for everyone and used for personalized lifestyle decisions. Health professionals would understand the health implications of variations in genes and assist in establishing a personal guide for maximizing genetic health. Consumers would understand their personal health risks and take actions accordingly. Health insurers and employers would not penalize individuals whose genetic profile indicates a high risk for specific conditions but would instead encourage them to practice safe genetic health behaviors; they would develop worker empowerment programs similar to those currently recommended by OSHA. Computer programs could assist with encouraging these behavior changes by such mechanisms as the Computer As Persuasive Tool (CAPTology) [26]. Research results would be translated into action quickly instead of the multi-year delay currently experienced [27]. However, to achieve this rosy vision of the future would require many changes.

1) This future requires understanding by all parties of how to deal with risks and probabilities; the US education system will be challenged to achieve this.
2) This future requires readable, tailored risk profiles generated for each individual; the scientific community will be challenged to determine the significance of the data, and the health care practitioners will be challenged understanding them.
3) This future requires time for providers and patients to discuss complicated information; the U.S. health care industry will be challenged to make this possible.
4) This future requires accurate on-line information resources; the consumer health information providers will be challenged to create this.
5) This future requires online information filtering skills of both providers and consumers; the educational system is challenged to teach this.
6) This future requires consumers with extensive health literacy; the educational system and our culture will both be challenged by this.

Many more requirements are also implied. Clearly the road will not be an easy one or a fast one to travel.

Table 2. Twelve Points of a Possible EMR Genomic Future

1. Universal, whole genome sequencing will take 10-15 years to appear.
2. Sequence data will appear in the EMR one gene at a time.
3. Specific gene testing panels will become common in the form of FDA-regulated kits focused on the detection of specific sets of mutations and later full sequences.
4. Full sequences will be stored in a newly developed component of the EMR.
5. Genetic meta-data from tests will be stored in the laboratory system, most likely the molecular diagnostic system.
6. EMR alerts will work by processing the laboratory meta-data with other patient data such as the specific medications being ordered.
7. The primary care physician will team-up with trusted Internet health sites to help patients understand the genetic and health implications.
8. Ultimately, the genome record will be generated at (or before) birth as part of routine newborn screening programs.
9. The parents receive their child's genetic risk analysis shortly after newborn screening. They discuss this not only with their pediatrician but with special health units established to help patients deal with questions.
10. The patient "owns" the genomic module, but the state is his "steward" and stores the data securely. It is used by the health systems authorized by the patient.
11. The genome record contains references to the "normal" sequence, its variants, and its health implications that are maintained in an international repository. The data structures, format, and stewardship regulations are governed by national and international standards.
12. The genetic risk analysis is updated routinely by intelligent "search agents," software programs validated by national and international panels of experts. These agents check the individual genome against the international repository to see if there is new knowledge that applies to this person.

3.2 Impact of Genome Data on Other e-Health Information Systems

The EMR will not be the only system profoundly altered by the genomic revolution. All of the e-Health information systems will be affected. It is perhaps superfluous to state that privacy issues will be paramount and generate much debate for many years. The discussion of other e-Health systems will focus on the various levels of data being stored. The initial discussion of the genomic impact on these levels can be credited to Sanchez [28].

At the population level, genomic epidemiology databases will be maintained for public health concerns. Some of this has already occurred, with the information about specific variants of the anthrax genome stored as part of the investigation of the anthrax letters sent to various congressman and news agencies in 2001 [29]. Similar records are being stored to determine the zoonotic origin of the SARS virus and the spread among people. The dairy cattle herd records are being augmented to attempt to track bovine spongiform encephalopathy (mad-cow disease) across multiple countries, herds, and birth cohorts [30]. Also at the population record are newborn screening databases for which data are increasingly being generated by mass spectroscopy methods, permitting testing for many more disorders than when tests are administered individually. The National Health

System in the UK is proposing a pilot project aimed at the generation of full genetic sequence records for a cohort of newborns [25].

At the disease level, there will undoubtedly be major revisions of coding and naming of disorders based on new molecular classifications of diseases. Efforts are currently underway to augment CPT, SNOMED and LOINC codes to accommodate genetic testing. Clinical practice guidelines will include gene tests or gene therapy based on specific genotypes. Clinical trials will target specific subsets for testing with new pharmaceutical agents, resulting in a set of drugs that work more effectively with some genotypes than with others.

At the patient level, the electronic medical record will undoubtedly store genomic data in various forms. The previous section of this paper has described this fully.

For tissue and organ banks, the specifics of the donors and recipients will be stored as fully as possible with regard to relevant genes. To address the cellular level, there will be specific computer models with different genotypes depicted for the intelligent design of new drugs. For specific genes, there will be global repositories of data such as those held by the NCBI (National Center for Biotechnology Information) (http://www.ncbi.nlm.nih.gov/) and EBI (European Bioinformatics Institute) (http://www.ebi.ac.uk/) that will be linked to genomic databases and individual EMRs via health systems.

3.3 Impact of Genomics on the Consumer Health Movement

There is a continued barrage of genome information on many of the Internet health news systems. Within a month's time in 2003, there were many stories pertaining to specific genes and their health implications. Example headlines include, "gene mutation may cause heart failure" (the PLN gene) [31], "study links binge eating to mutation in a gene" (the MC4R gene) [32], "genes explain why pain hurts more for some" (the COMT gene) [33], and "gene type cuts risk of bleeding after surgery" (the F5-Leiden gene) [34]. For consumers who wish to find information about their health condition and the genetic details as well, they can access the Genetics Home Reference (http://ghr.nlm.nih.gov/ghr/page/Home) from the National Library of Medicine; this system bridges the consumer health system MedlinePLUS as well as the database resources of the NCBI. Multiple systems are coordinated through the Genetics Alliance (http://www.geneticalliance.org/) and the National Office of Rare Diseases (NORD) (http://rarediseases.info.nih.gov/). At these sites, the motivated consumer can easily find chat rooms and listservs to help alleviate the isolation that was previously experienced by those with rare disorders, and their families. The consumer health movement is a societal force that holds promise to assist both with the education needs and the individual questions that will undoubtedly arise from genomic medicine.

4. The Future of e-Health and Genomic Medicine

Genomic health care holds the promise of optimal individual health maintenance and disease prevention. However, to realize this future, patients will primarily be asked to make behavior modifications based on discussions of risks and probabilities. This is a markedly different type of discussion than usually occurs today in health care. It will take a transformation of many aspects of health care to achieve this optimal future. E-Health systems will play an instrumental role in achieving this future, and will be pushed in directions not part of traditional informatics. E-Health systems will be instrumental in helping to manage the "information overload" of the HGP health implications. They can promote empowered managed care in the best sense. In fact, e-Health systems will be the enabler of these changes. Genomic medicine could not be fully realized without the systems being developed as part of the major changes stemming from the e-Health movement.

Acknowledgements

Candace Garb for editorial assistance; Douglas R. Mitchell, MD for critical review; and Mark Hoffman, PhD for stimulating discussion.

References

[1] Collins FS, Green ED, Guttmacher AE, Guyer MS. A vision for the future of genomics research. Nature 2003;422:835-47.

[2] Hood L. Systems biology: integrating technology, biology, and computation. Mechanisms of Ageing & Development 2003;124(1):9-16.

[3] De Moor GJ. Towards individualized health management: the importance of biomedical information sciences. Methods Inf Med. 2003;42(2):IV-VI.

[4] Guttmacher AE, Collins FS. Genomic medicine – a primer. N Engl J Med 2002;347(19):1512-20.

[5] Garrod AK. The incidence of Alkaptonuria: a study in chemical individuality. Lancet 1902, 2:1616-1620.

[6] Granadino B, Beltran-Valero de Bernabe D, Fernandez-Canon JM, Penalva MA, Rodriguez de Cordoba S. The human homogentisate 1,2-dioxygenase (HGO) gene. Genomics. 1997:Jul 15;43(2):115-22.

[7] Waldholz M. Genetic testing hits the doctor's office. The Wall Street Journal Online, December 3, 2003. www.djreprints.com.

[8] Evans WE. Pharmacogenomics: marshalling the human genome to individualise drug therapy. Gut 2003;52(suppl II):ii10-ii18.

[9] Guan, Min-Xin, et al. A biochemical basis for the inherited susceptibility to aminoglycoside ototoxicity. Human Molecular Genetics 2000;9(12):1787-1793.

[10] Hutchin T, et al. Prevalence of mitochondrial DNA mutations in childhood/congenital onset non-syndromic sensorineural hearing impairment. Am J Med Genet 2001;38:229-231.

[11] Anonymous. FDA clears new lab test to help predict those at risk of coronary heart disease. AWHONN Lifelines. 7(5):457-60, 2003 Oct-Nov.

[12] Omenn GS. Genetic advances will influence the practice of medicine: examples from cancer research and care of cancer patients. Genet. Med. 2002, 4;(6 Suppl):15S-20S.

[13] Williams RS, Willard HF, Snyderman R. Editorial: Personalized Health Planning. Science, 2003;300:549.

[14] Matthews AW. FDA issues rules on new era of 'personalized medicine.' The Wall Street Journal Online, November 3, 2003. http://online.wsj.com.

[15] Mansfield E. Genetic testing and personalized medicine: an FDA view. Preclinica, 2003;1(4):155-158.

[16] Anonymous. FDA Issues Guidance on Pharmacogenomics Data. FDA News release P03-89, November 3, 2003. The release may be viewed at http://www.fda.gov/bbs/topics/NEWS/2003/NEW00969.html

[17] McCabe LL, McCabe ERB. Direct-to-consumer genetic testing: access and marketing. Genetics in Medicine, 2004;6(1):58-59.

[18] American College of Medicine Genetics Board of Directors. ACMG statement on direct to consumer genetic testing. Genetics in Medicine, 2004;6(1):60.

[19] Burke A. Genomics gets personal. [Editor's Letter] Genome Technology 2003;39:7.

[20] Hawkins T. NIEHS and UNC to Collaborate on Registry of 20,000 Subjects to Relate Gene Variants and Environmental Disease. NIEHS Press Release, 2004: Jan 12.

[21] Personal communication, February 2004 – Johns Hopkins University Genetics Testing Laboratory.

[22] Pope, J., Associated Press. Tiny steps toward the $1,000 gene map. Kansas City Star, September 19, 2003. http://www.kansascity.com/mld/kansascity/business/6757124.htm.

[23] Mehnert R, Cravedi K. The Health Information Prescription. NLM Press Release, 2003: March 18.

[24] Mitchell JA, Fun J, McCray AT: Design of Genetics Home Reference: a new NLM consumer health resources. J Am Med Inform Assoc, submitted for publication, 2004.

[25] Department of Health White Paper. Our inheritance, our future: realising the potential of genetics in the NHS. [Summary] Department of Health, National Health Service, 2003. www.doh.gov.uk/genetics/whitepaper.htm.

[26] Chan AS. Health Captology: The Use of Persuasive Technologies in Healthcare Applications. Presented at the e-health conference "e-Health: Current Status and Future Trends in the EU and the US" February 12-13, 2004, Columbia, Missouri. http://www.hmi.missouri.edu/ehealth.

[27] Balas EA, Boren SA. Managing Clinical Knowledge for Health Care Improvement. Yearbook of Medical Informatics 2000:65-70.

[28] Sanchez FM. Bioinformatics and health: impacts of the Human Genome Project on Health Informatics. Upgrade, 2001, 2(1):36-43.

[29] Fraser CM. A Genomics-Based Approach to Biodefence Preparedness. Nature Reviews Genetics. 2004:5(1):23-44.

[30] Veneman AM: Ensuring a Health Food Supply. USDA Press Release. Keynote Address to the Agricultural Outlook Forum 2004: 2004: February 19.

[31] Associated Press. Gene Mutation may cause heart failure. CNN.com; http://www.cnn.com/2003/HEALTH/conditions/02/28/heart.gene.ap/.

[32] Anonymous. Study links binge eating to mutation in a gene. Associated Press, March 19, 2003.

[33] McCook A. Genes explain why pain hurts more for some. Reuters Health, February 20, 2003. http://www.nlm.nih.gov/medlineplus/.

[34] Carroll L. Gene type cuts risk of bleeding after surgery. Reuters Health, MEDLINEplus, February 24, 2003. http://www.nlm.nih.gov/medlineplus/.

E-Health: Current Status and Future Trends
G. Demiris (Ed.)
IOS Press, 2004

Privacy Enhancing Techniques in E-Health: An Overview

Georges J.E. DE MOOR[a], Brecht CLAERHOUT[b]
[a]*Department of Medical Informatics and Statistics, University Gent, Belgium*
[b]*CUSTODIX nv, Belgium*

Abstract. This overview highlights the relevance of Privacy Enhancing Techniques (PETs) in the context of e-Health. A number of validated privacy protecting techniques is briefly presented. The implementation of such PETs could provoke, for a number of applications, a shift in paradigm, namely from "Privacy through Security" to "Security through Privacy".

Keywords

Confidentiality of Data; Privacy of Persons; Trusted Third Parties (TTPs); Privacy Enhancing Techniques (PETs); e-Health; HealthGrid

1 Introduction

The increasingly intensive use of the Internet and the growing interest in Information and Communication Technology (I.C.T.) are providing numerous opportunities to exchange, store and process data, as well as a multitude of benefits to a wide range of professional sectors. In the coming years, electronic commerce (e-commerce), electronic health (e-health) and electronic government (e-government) will gradually become part of the day-to-day life.

However, because medical (and genetic) data are personal and/or highly sensitive, this major expansion in electronic information exchange raises serious concerns about privacy and info-ethics [1].

Cases involving health data being disclosed to third parties have repeatedly hit the headlines and have played a major role in developing a sense of mistrust among citizens and patients.

As the practice of genomic medicine develops, researchers and healthcare providers may want to store genetic profiles to determine treatment modalities as the need arises. The existence of such genetic databases will even increase the risk that unauthorized persons will obtain access.

When not adequately addressed or managed, such concerns can render individuals reluctant to share information and dissuade organizations from investing in innovative electronic services, thus undermining the potential for useful and more efficient e-services (e.g. research, quality assessment, market analysis, direct-to-consumers information, management-data studies etc.). Clinicians, researchers and other stakeholders will therefore need to safeguard the confidentiality of such sensitive patient information.

Protecting human rights (e.g. privacy) while maximizing research productivity is one of the current challenges. Well-intentioned privacy laws should not clash with the legitimate use of information when clearly to the public's benefit.

As innovative Privacy Enhancing Techniques (PETs) are now becoming available they offer tangible solutions to privacy protection matters, which therefore, should no longer be perceived as unsolvable obstacles.

2 Background

Privacy includes the right of individuals and organizations to determine for themselves when, how and to what extent information about them is communicated to others.

At one end of the spectrum of identifiability, data are completely anonymous and not linked to any identifiers. This is the least sensitive type of information. However, depending on how the anonymization process is carried out, some risk may remain for the anonymized data to be re-identified (e.g. through processes such as data matching) [2].

Next in the spectrum, identifying data are transformed into pseudo-identifiers, i.e. identifiers that cannot be linked to any real person or organization. In terms of privacy, this type of data may be viewed as equivalent, as far as sensitivity is concerned, to completely anonymous data, depending on the cryptographic techniques being used (cf. the irreversibility issue, see further).

Further down the spectrum, is the code-linked information where the identifiers are replaced with a code that, whenever necessary, can be linked to information that reveals the individuals' identities. From a privacy standpoint, and depending on how the codes used to re-identify the data are created (e.g. with simple conversion tables) and controlled, this information is more sensitive than completely anonymous data or than de-identified data linked to pseudo-identities.

Finally, at the opposite end of the spectrum is the completely identifiable information. From a privacy perspective, this is the most sensitive type of information, which is associated to the greatest risk.

A couple of basic approaches to safeguarding confidentiality have been identified in the past. The first approach focuses on the creators and maintainers of the information, prohibiting them from disclosing the information to inappropriate parties. An alternative approach focuses on the use, e.g. by Trusted Third Parties (TTPs) of so called Privacy-Enhancing-Techniques (PETs) and other measures using cryptographic techniques. In contrast with horizontal types of data exchange (e.g. for direct care), vertical communication scenarios (e.g. in the context of disease management studies and other research) do not require identities as such: here the use of pseudo-IDs can help find solutions.

Privacy enhancing solutions range from very simple to complex technical and non-technical methods and measures.

3 Trusted Third Parties and Pseudonymization as an Example of PET

One of the best known PETs used for data collection is probably pseudonymization. Pseudonymization refers to a specific Privacy Enhancing Technique used to withdraw and replace the true identities of individuals or organizations; contrary to simple de-identification, it still enables the linkage of data associated to the pseudo-identities (pseudo-IDs).

Pseudonymisation is a powerful and secure solution to the problem of reconciling the two following conflicting requirements:

- the adequate protection of individuals and organizations with respect to their identity and privacy;

- the ability to link the data associated with the pseudo-IDs, irrespective of the collection time and place (this being important in e.g. longitudinal studies).

Simply put, pseudonymisation translates a given identifier into a pseudo-identifier (a.k.a. 'digital pseudonym'). This is preferably done by using secure, dynamic and irreversible cryptographic techniques (and not static translation tables). The choice between an irreversible versus a reversible approach depends on users' needs.

Generated pseudonyms are thus represented by (to an observer) complete random selections of characters (letters, numbers and/or other marks). It is a flexible technique which can be employed in different ways, e.g. the transformation method can be time-related (a given identifier can always map with the same pseudo-ID or every time with a different pseudo-ID, the transformation method can change at specified time-intervals, ...) [4]. Careless use of pseudonymisation technology could lead to a false feeling of privacy protection. Special attention should be paid to the following aspects:

- Identifiers and assessment data (payload data) should be separated correctly. The separation should be done in such a way that the payload data do not contain fields that could lead to "indirect re-identification" (meaning re-identification of anonymous records by use of the database information content, not derived from listed identifiers). Implementation of pseudonymization technology should therefore be preceded by careful privacy risk assessment (see further);
- The identifier transformation process itself should not be performed with translation tables, but preferably with (when needed irreversible) cryptographic algorithms.Reversibility can be accepted (even required) in some cases, but has to be well controlled (both by policy and technical precautions);
- The algorithms used for pseudonymisation should be collision free (no synonyms in pseudonymous codes), robust and produce meaningless (e.g. not sequential) outputs.

Another question is whether the de-identification procedure should be performed with or without the help of a Trusted Third Party (TTP).

Trusted Third Parties or TTPs have in common that they provide as independent intermediaries "trust services" to other parties. When the security solution is based on pseudonymisation, the trustee is a pseudonymisation TTP. Proper and secure pseudonymisation can be performed with the support of such a pseudonymisation trust service provider, whose main features are:

- its strict independence as an organization;
- its strict code of conducts, trust practice statement and secrecy agreement policy.
- the trustworthiness of its methods, implementations and infrastructure;
- its adherence to the principles of openness and transparency regarding its methods;
- the provision of professional expertise related to the domain of relevance;
- its project-specific privacy and security policies;
- its documentation, operating reporting and auditing systems.

There are circumstances where the data collecting organizations are trustful by themselves: privacy protection can, in such cases, be organized without the direct involvement of a third party, but through the use of well designed privacy protection engines.

4 A Theoretical Approach of Privacy Protection

Correct use of privacy enhancing technology is impossible without proper background understanding of privacy protection and re-identification. In order to obtain such knowledge, a rigorous formalization of (re-)identification risks and privacy threats is needed. Different models based on statistics and information theory, exist. Privacy Gauging can be defined as *"measuring the risk that a subject in a 'privacy protected' database can be re-identified without cooperation of that subject or against his/her will"*.

We have developed a general framework for such analysis based on a generic model of re-identification attacks. In it highest level of abstraction, it consists of three major entities:

1. The anonymous database (de-identified database)
   This is the database containing anonymous records. It lists data of unknown subjects. It is the source containing possible sensitive information, which should not be disclosed.
2. The attacker
   The attacker is the entity aiming at deriving identities from the information kept in the anonymous database. In order to achieve his goal, he needs to link the anonymous data with real-world persons.
3. The observations database
   A database composed by the attacker, containing nominative information.

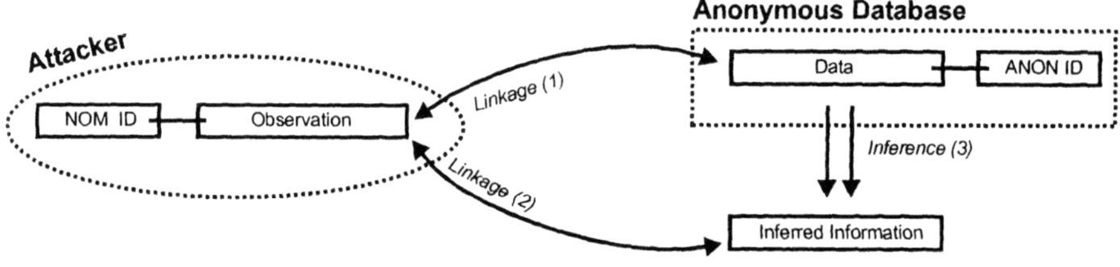

Figure 1. Generic Model for Database Privacy Analysis

The attacker composes this latter database out of 'observations' relevant for an attack. These nominative observations may be derived from different sources, such as :

- Information gathered from existing nominative databases;
- Social engineering: gathering information one is normally not entitled to, e.g. by exploiting social contacts;
- Factual data: e.g. data gathered by observations strictu senso.

'Relevant' (for an attack) means that the gathered information has to be related to the content of the anonymous database.

Although this model seems a too simplistic representation of reality, it can, thanks to its generic nature, be refined to such a level of complexity, that it encloses all relevant real-life aspects of re-identification and privacy protection. Based on this model, both theoretical calculations can be performed or practical algorithms implemented.

Privacy risk assessment or privacy gauging can be considered or used:

- as a research tool, providing a theoretical and scientific background for Privacy Enhancing Techniques, of particular interest when developing new ones;
- for a-priori privacy risk assessment in order to estimate the privacy risks before any data is collected and to specify the requirements for the protection measures to be implemented;
- for a-posteriori privacy risk assessment, which refers to the evaluation of existing databases (PET performance), and used as feedback for the theoretical models;
- as a Privacy Enhancing Technique for continuous monitoring of privacy risks.

5 Privacy Enhancing Techniques

Protecting the right to privacy, while optimizing e-applications, is a challenge that can be met with advanced Privacy Enhancing Techniques (PETs). Privacy Enhancing Technologies (PETs) can be defined as protocols, standards, and tools that directly assist in protecting privacy, minimizing the collection of personally identifiable information, and eliminating when possible, the collection of personally identifiable information [4].

A first type of PETs eliminates or minimizes the collection of personally identifiable data while still enabling the person in question to engage in a transaction or in communication (sending mail, doing a purchase, surfing the web, etc.). These techniques protect the individual privacy when a person is operating or communicating. In such scenarios, the person whose privacy is to be protected, remains more or less in control of the situation.

Another category covers a variety of PETs that are usually less under the direct control of the person to be protected. These techniques are often used for protecting identities in data collection. The goal is here to preserve the privacy of the persons who are the subjects of the information gathering, while still making useful information available for further processing. The nature of such type of PETs is well reflected by another definition of PETs: "A coherent system of ICT measures that protects privacy by eliminating or reducing personal data or by preventing unnecessary and/or undesired processing of personal data, all without losing the functionality of the information system" [5].

The choice of one or more techniques will largely depend on the context and the finality of the data handling and operations. As such, privacy protection applications are often designed to meet the specific needs of different organizations. To cite a few techniques:

- Hard de-identification, i.e. the complete removal of identifying information from the dataset at the source side by the owner of the data. If this is properly implemented, the data must no longer be considered personal and privacy protection no longer applies;

- Various types of anonymization and/or pseudonymization that (ir-)reversibly change identifiers into random pseudo-identifiers, preferably using cryptographic techniques (it should be clear that these techniques - in their simplest form - do not suffice to de-identify data). Several variants exist:
  - the de-identification may be reversible or irreversible;
  - conducted with or without the help of a Trusted Third Party (TTP);
  - in a batch or in an interactive mode, etc.;

- Controlled database perturbation or transformation: perturbation is a concept known from the field of statistical databases. One tries hereby to maintain the statistical characteristics of the data while removing the specific characteristics of individual records, by:
  - modifying record values;
  - swapping values between records;
  - adding fake data (dilution);

It remains however difficult to maintain the control over the correctness of the extracted information and the adequate protection of privacy. It can easily be understood that privacy protection by use of database perturbation, if not performed under a well-controlled way, can render a database useless for data analysis techniques such as association rule mining. , Less drastic methods such as generalisation are therefore more commonly used;

- Data flow segmentation: refers to the spreading of collected (pseudonymized) data over several databases. There are different methods to do this, e.g. data variables can be split up among databases, or data subjects can be grouped in different databases based on certain criteria. Segmentation techniques limit the amount of indirect identifying data by spreading them. The rationale behind such measure is that not all research data need to be accessible by all and at the same time;

- Diagnostic (e.g. preventive) privacy protection gauging of databases to calculate direct and indirect (re-)identification risks. Privacy gauging is often a prerequisite for the correct choice and configuration of PETs (including determining which PETs to use with which parameters);

- Privacy enhancing software agents (a framework of) that interact intelligently to continuously check and ensure the privacy protection in a database;

- The use of proxy services to mask IP addresses.

The above list of PETs is far from complete. The goal was not to provide an exhaustive list of all the existing privacy protection techniques, nor to give a detailed description of each single technique.

6 A Look into the Future: Preserving the Privacy in a HealthGrid Environment

The promise of the HealthGrid is to allow to store, access and process large amounts of data by sharing resources and tools in a virtual distributed environment. Mass storage systems, high performance computational platforms and other distributed Grid resources will become interlinked and will offer through intelligent middleware, a whole series of new co-operative and collaborative services.

The Grid will thus act as a single computer at the users' disposal. With the Grid technology removing a number of barriers between local and remote resources, a whole range of new communication scenarios will emerge and will have to be re-analyzed in an e-Health and e-Security context. Of course, new measures will have to be put in place to prevent unauthorized actions and when needed, to preserve the confidentiality of the data.

The first initiatives applying Grid technologies in Health have covered fields as medical digital imaging (including simulations and reconstructions), DNA sequence analysis, protein pattern identification and more general database knowledge extraction (e.g. in order to provide guidelines to health professionals or decision support data to planners). Other collaboration examples include medical problem solving environments, screening programmes (e.g. mammographic screening), large clinical trials, e-learning, knowledge discovery and the interconnection of advanced diagnostic centres and health providers allowing for remote diagnosis or other telemedicine services.

Today's Grid security models do not provide complete solutions. The implementation of more advanced Privacy Enhancing Techniques (PETs) will thus more than likely have to complement the more conventional security approaches since the data in a HealthGrid (e.g. the medical and genetic data) are often highly sensitive.

It is important that the one who makes sensitive data available to third parties (sharing in this case on a Grid) keeps full control of the amount of information that is disclosed. Therefore, external access to the data from the Grid could be managed by a local Privacy Protecting Interface. Such an interface could not only implement a pseudonymization system (by converting patients' identities into pseudo-identities) but also filter the data to remove or modify any other identifying information and evaluate the database- requests themselves ("query filtering"). Using such a local interface (agent) would allow the data provider, who is ultimately responsible for the exposed data, to remain in full control of what is shared on the Grid [6].

7 Conclusions

PETs should be considered complementary to the more conventional security approaches, whereby confidentiality of data is being protected through mechanisms such as identification, authentication, access control, encryption etc. The paradigm shift presented here can be summarized as 'privacy through security' being replaced/complemented by 'security through privacy'.

Protecting civil rights (e.g. privacy) while maximizing e.g. research productivity is one of the coming challenges for the next decade. A first step towards this objective is the research and implementation of Privacy Enhancing Techniques that provide means to unlock invaluable data sources for the benefit of society without endangering individual privacy.

References

[1] De Moor GJE, Claerhout B, De Meyer F. Privacy Enhancing Techniques: the Key to Secure Communication and Management of Clinical and Genomic Data. Methods Inf Med. 2003;42(2):148-153.

[2] Quantin C, Binquet C, Allaert FA. Decision Analysis for the Assessment of a Record Linkage Procedure: Application to a Perinatal Network. International Journal of Medical Informatics 2004; (in press).

[3] De Meyer F, Claerhout B, De Moor G. The PRIDEH project: taking up Privacy Protection Services in e-Health. Proceedings of MIC 2002 "Health Continuum and Data Exchange". IOS Press, 2002; p. 171-177.

[4] Agrawal R. Why is P3P not a PET. Submission to the W3C Workshop on the Future of P3P, 12-13 Nov. 2002; Dulles,Virginia,USA.
Available from: http://www.w3.org/2002/p3p-ws/pp/epic.pdf

[5] Borking et al.. Privacy-Enhancing Technologies: the Path to Anonymity. Information and Privacy Commissioner Ontario Canada and Registratiekamer, The Netherlands, 1995.

[6] De Moor G, Claerhout B. Privacy Protection for Healthgrid Applications. Method Inf Med. 2004; (in press)

E-Health: Current Status and Future Trends
G. Demiris (Ed.)
IOS Press, 2004

Health Captology – Application of Persuasive Technologies to Health Care

Albert S. CHAN, MD
Stanford Medical Informatics
Department of Family and Community Medicine,
University of California, San Francisco School of Medicine
USA

Abstract. Professionals in industries such as advertising and sales have used techniques of persuasion to enhance the efficacy of marketing campaigns and sales revenues. In contrast, health care has traditionally relied on the persuasive power of facts and evidence to encourage healthy behavior. The evidence suggests, however, that this current approach is failing. Health care experts and opinion leaders cite overwhelming evidence of an epidemic in diseases such as obesity and diabetes, despite numerous initiatives to educate the public how to prevent morbidity and mortality. Health captology, the application of persuasive technology to health care, attempts to leverage proven persuasive techniques to improve clinical outcomes.

Introduction

Our common sense experience indicates that it is often hard to do the right thing when it comes to our health and the practice of healthcare. For example, analysis of the National Health and Nutrition Examination Survey (NHANES) 1999-2000 reveals a national obesity epidemic. 64.5% of all Americans are obese or overweight, resulting in over 300,000 deaths annually. [1] As a primary care physician, I am often tasked with convincing my patients to pursue healthy behaviors such as eating properly and increasing exercise. Unfortunately, it is clear that in general, health care professionals are losing the battle against largely preventable diseases such as obesity and the associated complications such as cardiovascular disease and diabetes.

Patients are not the only population that finds difficulty following proper behaviors. Despite widely-available, evidence-based guidelines for highly prevalent diseases such as hypertension, studies have generally reported very poor rates of adherence to these best practices. The consequences for non-adherence are considerable – poorly treated hypertension greatly increase the risks of cardiovascular disease and death.

Why is it often difficult to do the right thing? Of course, the answer is complex and multi-factorial. However, it is apparent that compliance professionals, individuals such as advertisers and salespeople who professionally seek to influence people, have at their disposal powerful weapons that may be used to promote unhealthy behaviors. These tools may provide much more compelling or persuasive messages that overpower the fact-based information traditionally provided in the health care domain.

In Influence: Science and Practice, psychologist Robert Cialdini systematically explores the theory and practice of persuasion. He codifies six principles – reciprocation, consistency, social proof, liking, authority, and scarcity – that are used by compliance professionals to influence people. When invoked, these principles activate fixed action patterns of behavior which can be exploited to bring about desired behaviors [2]. We will explore how these principles are used by various interests to exploit humans, citing examples provided by Cialdini and others. Then, we will attempt to relate how these principles may be used to bring about better healthcare outcomes.

Persuasion Principles

Reciprocation

"There is no such thing as a free lunch" – Milton Freedman

Reciprocation is a heuristic that we are taught at a very early age. It simply states that we should seek to repay gifts or favors given to us by others. For example, if we receive a holiday card from someone, we are likely to send a card in return. This rule of thumb is particularly useful for building communities, as it encourages sharing between others and the development of symbiotic relationships.

However, by extension, the rule of reciprocity can invoke an obligation to repay gifts or favors to us. It is this sense of obligation that can be exploited to manipulate us to return gifts in situations which may be against our benefit. A classic example is the Hare Krishna Society, a religious sect which was well-known for soliciting donations in public places such as airports. The Krishna members were taught to give gifts to would-be donors, such as a flower or the Bhagavad Gita (Back to Godhead) magazine prior to soliciting donations, resulting wildly successful increase in fundraising.

Pharmaceutical companies use the principle of reciprocity with both patients and physicians to encourage use of their products. Traditionally, pharmaceutical representatives are tasked with introducing new products to physicians. Ranging from small gifts such as branded pens to lavish "educational" dinners, do these gifts affect physician choices and judgment about choice of medical therapy? 67% of faculty physicians & 77% of resident physicians felt that physicians could be compromised by interaction with pharmaceutical representatives [3]. Similarly, samples of new medications are given to patients to encourage brand loyalty and continued use of that particular brand of medication in the patient. Once limited to physician offices, pharmaceutical corporations are offering coupons for free sample medications directly to consumers in popular media, print ads, and on the Internet.

Consistency and Commitment

Generally, individuals are rewarded for maintaining consistency. In our society, consistent people are considered stable and reliable. Hence, the rule of consistency dictates that once an individual makes a choice, the internal pressure to remain consistent with that commitment will guide behavior.

Cialdini discusses a classic consumer example of this in the 1980s, the Cabbage Patch Kid. For years, the doll was the hottest selling toy at Christmas time and intentionally under- supplied at many retail stores. Attempting to honor the promise of the toy at Christmas, parents went to great lengths to either obtain the toy at exorbitant prices or bought the toy after Christmas (in addition to a gift purchased before Christmas). The after-Christmas sales of the Cabbage Patch Kid averaged $150 million for many years.

Many behavior management programs work under a similar principle. On an individual level, studies indicate that the mere mention of smoking cessation to patients by their physicians can result in a reduction in smoking. Similarly, Weight Watchers facilitates weight reduction by asking patients to commit to weekly "weigh-ins", forming a community of patients trying to lose weight. Participants are rewarded for continued participation and penalized for missing meetings by additional monetary fees. The sheer thought of these penalties help members maintain attendance.

Social proof

Social norms often shape the individual conceptions of realty. For example, from a very early age, we are taught by our parents to observe certain societal customs and etiquettes. Individuals who don't follow these norms are often looked at strangely, as if they somehow missed the cues that we are expected to understand. At the extreme, consider the case of patients with autism. Autistic children, unable to interpret the social cues that normal children use to understand situation and social interaction, have difficulty bonding or forming meaningful relationships with others.

Social proof is a technique we use as a mental shorthand, using social norms to guide our behavior. A classic example of social proof is the shared belief systems created by cults. Jim Jones and his People's Temple moved from San Francisco to Guyana, South America. In a mass demonstration of social proof, the cult members, including mothers and their children, committed mass suicide by drinking cyanide-laced Kool-Aid after the assignation of Leo Ryan, a California congressman who traveled to Jonestown to investigate the cult.

Print and television media use social proof to promote images of popularity and social acceptance for their products. A poignant example of this is the marketing of "fast foods" and "junk foods'. The fast food industry spent over $3 billion on ads targeting children alone. [4] These ads often portray happy children collectively enjoying a particular fast food product. A recent review of the scientific literature about childhood obesity by the Kaiser Family Foundation supports the conclusions that watching television is correlated with increases in childhood obesity and reducing that time leads to reductions in obesity. Interestingly, this increase in obesity is not simply a matter of replacing physical activity with television time; rather, it appears that the use of persuasive media images encourage unhealthy behaviors in children. [5]

Liking

This principle refers to the notion that we are more likely to listen to someone who we like and trust. In our personal experience, we have all met salespeople who strike up a conversation and try to find similarities. More than idle small talk, these compliance professionals are implementing a tried-and-true technique of liking to make the customer more amenable to potential sales presentations. For example, Mary Kay Cosmetics, Amway, and Tupperware Corporation are three companies that market directly to consumers by hosting parties at a friend's house.

An interesting tool to increase the likelihood that someone will like you - the use of compliments. Cialdini describes a car salesman named Joe Girard, whom has been called the world's greatest salesman by the Guinness Book of World Records. He would simply send out cards to his former customers 12 times a year with his name and the phrase, "I like you." Amazingly, even if individuals know that the praise may not be genuine or given with a secondary gain in mind, the praise still had a profound impact on the likeability of the individual delivering praise. [6]

Authority

Another shortcut that guides our behavior is to listen to our experts. Experts play an important role in our daily lives. Parents can provide lessons about life to their children. Ministers can provide spiritual guidance for those with religious beliefs. Financial planners can guide our financial decisions. Physicians provide advice to us about healthy behaviors. The power of our belief in authority figures, however, can be used by compliance professionals to subtly influence our behavior.

As an example, former football coach Mike Ditka is a spokesman for a recently released medication for erectile dysfunction. Ditka is not a world-renowned urologist or researcher on erectile dysfunction. Yet, his success as a powerful former athlete and coach in a sport that represents traditionally "manly" values of toughness and virility gives social acceptance to the use of medications for impotence.

An experiment by Stanley Milgrim demonstrated the extent to which we are willing to listen to our authority figures. Dr. Milgrim recruited study subjects, telling them they were participating in a study of the effects on punishment on learning and memory. Subjects were instructed to deliver shocks to a "student" who was in actuality an actor who simulated receiving electric shocks to improve performance on learning tasks. Milgrim's studies indicated that when prompted by an authority figure, the subject would continue to deliver shocks, even if the actor was pleading for the shocks to cease. [7]

Scarcity

The final weapon of influence that Cialdini discusses is the concept of scarcity – that is, if a commodity is perceived as not readily available, we perceive it as more valuable. Consider the pervasiveness of infomercials on television. One common theme is the use of the scarcity principle. For example, we have all heard the phrase, "If you call within the next half hour, you will receive a special [scarce] gift".

Amazon.com has a special feature on its website called "Gold Box". This feature offers customers 60 minutes to peruse 10 special items. Once the customer has decided not to purchase the item, that item and its "special savings" disappears *forever*. Also, the customer is only able to access the Gold Box *once* every twenty-four hours. Anecdotally, the Gold Box has been one of the most successful marketing efforts, continually increasing traffic to the site and bringing customers back to sample items available at Amazon.com.

Can Technology Persuade?

BJ Fogg has introduced the discipline of captology – computers as persuasive technologies. In his doctoral work, Fogg explored how computers can successfully apply the same persuasion techniques that are employed by human compliance professionals. An experimental proof of this is the Stanford Reciprocity Study. Subjects were presented with the task of ranking items in terms of their value for survival on a desert island. The experimental subjects were given helpful assistance from the computer to solve the task; control subjects did not receive such assistance. After receiving helpful advice, experimental subjects were more willing to perform a subsequent, seemingly unrelated task of building a color palette of human perception "for the computer" than the control group. [8]

Fogg discusses three roles that computers can fill as persuasive agents. First, computers can create a **medium** for safe experimentation and rehearsal of situations, and to explore the effects of actions in these simulations. Second, computers can serve as persuasive **tools** that assist individuals monitor their progress toward the appropriate outcome measure. These tools can add transparency to a disease process, making it easier to see and follow the data. Third, computers are potential **social actors,** providing the same support and reinforcement that a human can provide. [9]

In these roles, Fogg outlines six distinct features where computers have distinct advantages over human persuaders:

1. Computers are more persistent than human beings, never tiring or giving up
2. Computers allow anonymity
3. Computers have store, access, and analyze large volumes of data
4. Computers can use multiple modalities, including rich audio-visual media
5. Computer software can scale and grow as demand increases
6. Computers can be ubiquitous, such as applications available on the Internet.

An example of how the tools of captology are utilized is the online game, America's Army. America's Army is an online experience of what it is like to join the Army. The game provides a medium in which prospective soldiers (potential recruits) can simulate rising up the ranks from basic training up to the level of Green Beret. "Special Forces Stats" and training tasks in marksmanship give the user tools to measure their progression in skills training. Finally, the game reinforces a "job well done" with compliments from the computerized commanding officer. At $8M in development costs, America's Army has become one of the U.S. Army's most cost-effective recruiting tools, contributing to the fourth year in a row that the Army has met its recruitment goals.

Health Captology – The Application of Persuasive Technologies to Healthcare

Instead of using persuasive technologies to sell goods or convince people to eat unhealthy foods, **health captology** studies how persuasive principles can be utilized to promote healthy behaviors. By understanding the science and practice of persuasion, users of health captology can create more compelling, convincing messages to promote better clinical outcomes.

Applications of Health Captology for Patients

Three important factors contribute to successful clinical outcomes (Figure 1). Patients need to understand the rationale behind the disease through education. Tools help patients facilitate the measurement of their progress toward the goal. Support systems provide necessary encouragement for continued efforts to managing disease effectively. By answering these three needs, health captology can empower patients to become better advocates for their own health care.

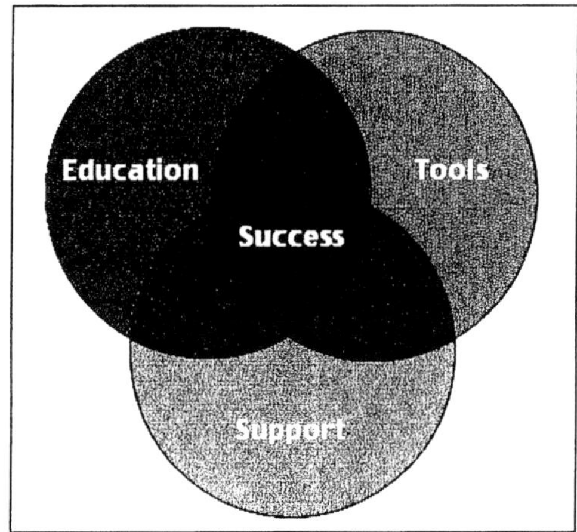

Figure 1.

Education

Patient understanding of the nature of their illness is one factor that contributes to a lasting commitment to behavior change.

Simulations are one example of how computers can act as persuasive media. In simulations, patients can safely trial how their actions are causally related to the outcome.

HIV Roulette is a simulation of the health risks involved in sexual activity located at the San Francisco Exploratorium. Based on real data from San Francisco, CA, users select various characteristics about potential sexual partners including IV drug use, partner history of sexual behavior, and protected vs. unprotected sexual intercourse and play the game until they contract HIV. The simulation thus provides a safe environment to learn about the factors that influence risk of contracting disease.

Baby-Think-It-Over Program is a curriculum that is designed to help prevent teen pregnancy. Teens are asked to carry a doll, RealCare Baby II, which simulates the needs of an infant. A study of 150 adolescents that participated in the Baby-Think-It-Over curriculum reported that 95% of the teens felt they were not ready to be parents. [10]

Tools

Activity monitors such as SportBrain or PAM encourage increases in physical activity by tracking the number of steps walked each day. This data can provide additional motivation to meet target goals, such as walking 10,000 steps per day.

In the disease of diabetes, proper monitoring requires painful blood sampling via finger stick and interpretation of blood glucose data. Adherence to testing is poor in both adults and children, leading to poor management of the disease. GlucoWatch is a product that reads the blood glucose transdermally, reducing a painful barrier to obtaining blood glucose data. Also, GlucoWatch facilitates the analysis of interpretation of blood glucose data with computer generated summaries of the data.

Support

Quitnet.com is a web site designed to assist patients stop smoking. Similar to Weight Watchers and Alcoholics Anonymous, Quitnet utilizes persuasion principles such as social proof and consistency/commitment to provide a supportive online community. Quitnet's online forums and chat rooms give tips from how others deal with the trials of smoking cessation. Testimonials from other successful clients model a healthy life without smoking. Quitnet also applies the technique of consistency/commitment by publicly announcing the users' quit date and anniversaries to encourage adherence to this healthy lifestyle. Unlike a human, Quitnet is dependably available 24 hours a day, seven days a week to provide remedies to the craving for nicotine.

Bringing it all together

eDiets.com is a website that exemplifies many of the concepts we have discussed. eDiets.com helps users build a personalized weight loss and fitness plan, including consideration of religious and food preferences, and complicating health conditions. The online presence provides a level of anonymity to overcome concerns such as embarrassment or shyness that may inhibit patients going to traditional communities. A professional dietician is a trusted authority figure, providing credibility to the advice provided on the site. Representative individuals from all demographic groups offer social proof in the form of powerful narratives detailing how they used eDiets successfully. Interactive discussions educate users about the benefits of weight loss and exercise. Tools such as an automatically-generated shopping list and graphical updates of your daily weight loss progress facilitate adherence to the weight loss plan. Finally, the community continually provides the online support from fellow users and weight loss experts.

Applications of Health Captology for Physicians

Physicians are not immune to the persuasive forces and workflow demands that sometimes discourage ideal practice patterns. A common example of this is the treatment of hypertension. The Joint National Committee on Prevention, Detection, Evaluation, and Treatment of High Blood Pressure (JNC) is a national expert panel that periodically disseminates practice guidelines discussing appropriate therapy for the treatment of hypertension. Despite the wide availability of these guidelines, adherence to the guideline is poor, as low as 11% in some studies [11]. Studies have revealed many barriers to guidelines adherence including insufficient awareness or familiarity of a guideline, ability to overcome the inertia of previous practice, and external barriers to perform recommendations such as time constraints [12].

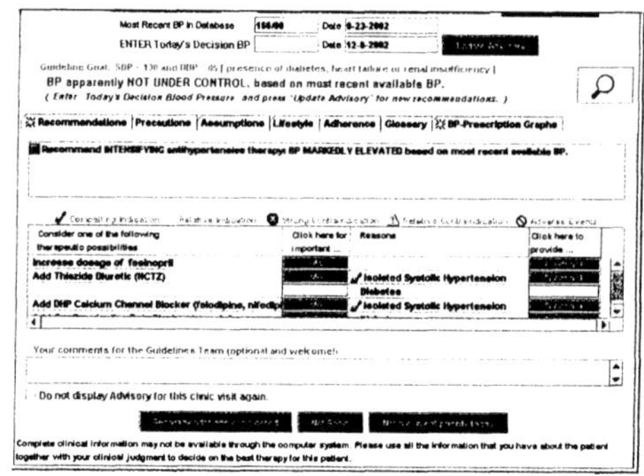

Figure 2. Sample ATHENA DSS recommendations

ATHENA DSS (Assessment and Treatment of Hypertension: Evidence-Based Automation Decision Support System) is a guideline-based decision support system for the treatment of hypertension that attempts to address some of these barriers. Based on widely accepted national guidelines for hypertension (JNC 6 and the Veterans Administration (VA)), ATHENA DSS delivers treatment advisories to clinicians at the point of care. ATHENA DSS acts this via an interface to the VA CPRS system, an electronic medical record in patient care delivery settings nationwide.

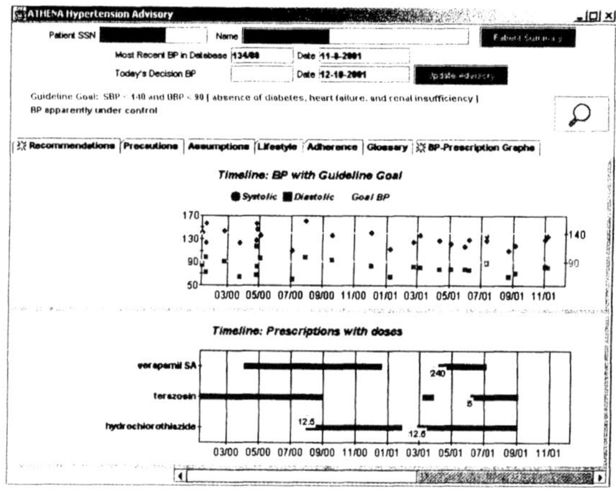

Figure 3. The BP – Prescription Graph displays blood pressure values associated with the patient's filling of prescriptions.

ATHENA DSS utilizes a number of persuasive techniques to encourage clinician adherence. ATHENA DSS operationalizes the guideline for clinical workflow, assisting the clinician quickly synthesize multiple considerations in the context of patient-specific clinical data. Also, clinician users of ATHENA DSS have ready access to the evidence from national experts and scientific literature that supports ATHENA DSS recommendations, adding credibility to the information. Finally, graphical tools (as depicted in figure 3) enable the clinicians to quickly see where changes in patient adherence to medical therapy affect blood pressure control [13,14].

Conclusions

Traditional methods of changing behaviors in healthcare have unfortunately enjoyed mixed success, even in the face of overwhelming evidence of the benefits of healthy behaviors. Leveraging the successful use of persuasive principles in other domains, **health captology,** the application of persuasive technologies to health care, provides new tools for practitioners seeking to improve clinical outcomes.

References

[1] U.S. Department of Health and Human Services. The Surgeon General's Call to Action to Prevent and Decrease Overweight and Obesity, 2001.

[2] Cialdini, RB, Influence: Science and Practice, Allyn and Bacon: Fourth Edition, 2001.

[3] McKinney, WP, et al, "Attitudes of internal medical faculty and residents towards professional interaction with pharmaceutical sales representatives", Journal of American Medical Association 264:13, October 3, 1990

[4] Harris Interactive, "The Market Influence and Power of Youth", *Trends and Tudes,* 3 (February 2004) 2, http://www.harrisinteractive.com/news/newsletters/k12news/HI_Trends&TudesNews2004_v3_iss02.pdf

[5] "The Role of Media in Childhood Obesity", Kaiser Family Foundation, Issue Brief: February 2004, http://www.kff.org/entmedia/loader.cfm?url=/commonspot/security/getfile.cfm&PageID=32022

[6] Drachman, D., deCarfel, A, Inkso, C.A. "The extra credit effect in interpersonal attraction", Journal of Experimental Psychology 14: 458-467.

[7] Milgrim, Stanley, Obedience to Authority., Harper & Row, 1974.

[8] Fogg, B.J., Charismatic Computers: Creating More Likeable and Persuasive Interactive Technologies by Leveraging Principles from Social Psychology, Doctoral Dissertation: Department of Communications,
Stanford University, 1997.

[9] Fogg, BJ, Persuasive Technology: Using Computers to Change What We Think and Do, Morgan Freeman, 2002

[10] Clark, B, "Baby-Think-It-Over Program: Changing teens' attitudes about parenting and parenthood", http://www.realityworksinc.com/cms_resources/596170aa-d6ed-462f-b75a-ea9589cf2796.pdf, October 29,1998.

[11] Pedone C, Lapane KL. "Generalizability of guidelines and physicians' adherence. Case study on the Sixth Joint National Committee's guidelines on hypertension", BMC Public Health. 3(1):24. July 21, 2003.

[12] Cabana MD, Rand CS, Powe NR, Wu AW, Wilson MH, Abboud PA, Rubin HR. "Why don't physicians follow clinical practice guidelines? A framework for improvement.", JAMA 282(15):1458-65, Oct 20, 1999

[13] Goldstein MK, Hoffman BB., Coleman RW, Musen MA, Tu SW, Advani A, Shankar R, O'Connor M, Implementing Clinical Practice Guidelines While Taking Account of Evidence: ATHENA, an Easily Modifiable Decision-Support System for Management of Hypertension in Primary Care. AMIA Annual Symposium, Los Angeles, CA, 2000: p. 303-304.

[14] Goldstein MK, Hoffman, BB, Coleman RW, Tu SW, Shankar RD, O'Connor M, Martins SB, Advani A, Musen MA, Patient Safety in Guideline-Based Deci-sion Support for Hypertension Management: ATHENA DSS. Journal of the American Medical In-formatics Association 2002. 9 (6 Suppl): p.S11-16

Speak-ER: An Audible Web-Based Medical Record for Emergency Patients

Francesco PINCIROLI[a,b,c,d], Emanuela CORBETTA[b], Matteo F. TAMBURINI[b], Andrea MATTASOGLIO[e], Stefano BONACINA[a,b,d], Marco MASSEROLI[a,b], Giovanni MELONI[e], Piergiorgio SPAGGIARI[f]

[a]Dipartimento di Bioingegneria, [b]Politecnico di Milano, Piazza Leonardo da Vinci 32, I-20133 Milano, Italy

[c] Centro per l'Ingegneria Biomedica del Consiglio Nazionale delle Ricerche, Via Golgi 39, I-20133 Milano, Italy

[d] MultiMedica Hospitals, Via Milanese 300, I-20099 Sesto San Giovanni (MI), Italy

[e] CILEA Inter-university Consortium for Information and Communication Technology, Via R. Sanzio 4, I-20090 Segrate - Milano, Italy

[f] Eugenio Morelli Hospital, Via Zubiani 33, I-23039 Sondalo(SO), Italy

Abstract. Emergency conditions can inhibit the use of clinical data, even when it has been professionally collected and structured. Our aim is to improve the assessment of patients' medical histories in emergency situations. Under emergency conditions, when it may be impractical for health care providers to interact with a visual display of patient data, a "speaking" medical record may be useful. We are investigating the use of a voice synthesizer in conjunction with MyAngelWeb®, an Italian web-based medical record service. Only the textual subset of patient medical records was considered and restructured according to the needs imposed by voice communication. The quality of the received messages was tested. Some quantitative features, including the number of words and time durations, were considered together with other subjective features, including intelligibility of single words and overall significance of the voice messages. Provided that the linguistic architecture of a medical records' text is arranged to minimize the number of choices presented to the user, and phrases are kept short with few acronyms, health care providers can satisfactorily interact with the service.. Audible medical record delivery may be considered as an effective enhancement to those datasets needed in emergencies.

Introduction

"Storing everything for the just retrieval of all we need, anywhere and anytime we need it". After some forty years, this phrase reasonably summarizes persistent unresolved problems in digital medical record management. The recent opening in the USA of the Medical Record Institute [1], and the quantity of funds the European Union gives to the subject [2] are significant signs of the problem relevance. Some difficulties arise from the wide variety of medical record user's and their varying roles in the provision of health care [3]. These many roles generate a wide spectrum of information needs and methods of retrieving medical records data. Satisfying such a variety demands a careful and highly structured medical record data entry process.

For example, the role-oriented granularity of medical record data presents a difficult and time consuming challenge. The classic information technology systems and concepts are insufficient [4]to address the variety of medical data types, where the major classes (alphanumeric texts, signals, and images) are very different from one another. The challenge is magnified by the health care providers' inherent need to integrate data in various data typesand from different sources. Even when the data sources stay within the same hospital, effective patient-centered organization of medical data is still a difficult task..

The spread of the Internet has great potential to change digital medical record management. The potential to deliver "anytime/anywhere" access to medical records, and to store any and all valuable data, seems tantalizingly close. However, the problem remains of retrieving all and only the relevant data we need at a given time.

The Internet does offer a novel means of addressing this problem by enabling patients to promote and help maintain their own digital medical record [5,6]. There are numerous barriers to such an approach, in particular the quality and focus of record content, privacy and security issues, data persistence, and host service continuity. Appendix 1 includes a recent summary of initiatives in the area of web-based personal digital medical record services.

For the patient at risk of emergency we already emphasized [5] that we do not believe in a web-based personal medical record prepared by the patient. For example, even if the patient has a role in making his digital medical record accessible online, in an emergency the health care provider may not have access to a computer terminal to view the record. However, it seems reasonable to ask in such a scenario if it might be feasible to "utter" vocally the medical history of the patient in a convenient and flexible manner? Specifically, could providers rely on listening to alphanumeric text of the digitally stored medical history delivered by telephone? In this chapter we describe our implementation of a speaking electronic medical record system, called "speak-ER", that attempts to giving speaking capabilities to a web-based medical record service using mobile telephony. We implemented this concept for MyAngelWeb®, a web-based digital medical record for the patient at risk of emergency [5,7].

1. Background

Mobile phones are already widespread. Moreover, mobile phones are usable almost anywhere. Appendix 2 gives a short summary of present basic aspects of mobile telephony and of emerging technologies and concepts. Multimedia PCs are already widespread too in private homes and offices, although to a lesser extent in the European Union than in the U.S.

Speak-ER was conceived to provide a properly prepared, web-based, personal digital medical record specifically designed to be automatically read and audibly delivered to a user. A mobile phone and a PC loudspeaker are both typical channels for delivering the message.

An audible medical record is not a new concept. Doctors frequently and satisfactorily discuss clinical cases over the telephone. It is true that the interactive nature of a conversation plays an important role in the effectiveness of telephone communications. Nevertheless, it may still be valuable for some communications to be carried by a machine, asynchronously. Provided that the clinical description of a patient is both prepared by a doctor and properly stored on a web server, it can be read automatically to great effect. When starting from alphanumerically recorded texts, a voice synthesizer can perform well. Even if the performance of current synthesizers is still imperfect, an ad-hoc experiment can reasonably be pursued. Starting from digitally pre-recorded audio files, a digital audio player can provide similar results.

The intellectual content of Medical Record paragraphs need not be different to accommodate a speaking medical record. By default, a clinical presentation of a patient in emergency conditions covers: a) Personal data; b) Presentation data; c) Past Diagnoses; d) Allergies; e) Adverse Reactions to Drugs; f) Vaccinations; g) Blood Group; h) Past Surgery Operations; i) Final Comments.

Speak-ER will require a different paragraph structure and style than it's the original incarnation of MyAngelWeb®. The traditional medical record is specifically designed for visual consumption, consisting of quickly navigable and browsable through text, graphics and images. However, the only one way to use a speaking medical record is to hear it with one's ears, listening to audible messages. This is a strictly mono-directional channel, which does not easily accommodate jumping around within the data, focusing, selecting, going back and forth and so on. Therefore, the new technology will require different technicalities. Perhaps more importantly, is that the new approach will require the user to adopt different interaction modalities, different levels of attention, even different behaviors. A general consequence is that the text of existing MyAngelWeb® medical records that were originally prepared to be viewed, have to be revised for speak-ER. Additional difficulties arise with acronyms, abbreviations, diseases, and drug names, all of which are more easily misunderstood in audible messages than in written ones.

2. Methods

2.1 Vocal Interaction Commands

By necessity, speak-ER's user interface is also audible. In such a case the fewer interactive commands and choices required for the user the better. The user should not be required to learn and remember sets of commands nor step through long lists of options. This is especially true in emergency conditions, when the attention of the health care provider should stay focused on the patient's condition..

Both the "Rewind" (in audiocassettes) and "Back" (in websites) features are "before" commands. However, they apply to different message architectures. "Rewind" is satisfactory for mono-dimensional information like spoken messages. Rewinding a tape is simply for hearing again what one has already heard. "Back" is needed for hierarchically structured or multidimensional information, where one may also want to return to examine previously discarded alternatives. The effective implementation of a full "Back" command on a purely vocal channel always raises user interaction problems.

2.2 Content Architecture for Vocal Fruition

Major differences in data structure between the original MyAngelWeb® style and the speak-ER style of medical records for the same patient are graphically summarized in Figure 1, where phone interaction is described as a state machine [8]. Each user made choice leads to a state change. Each state deals with a data file related to a piece of information.

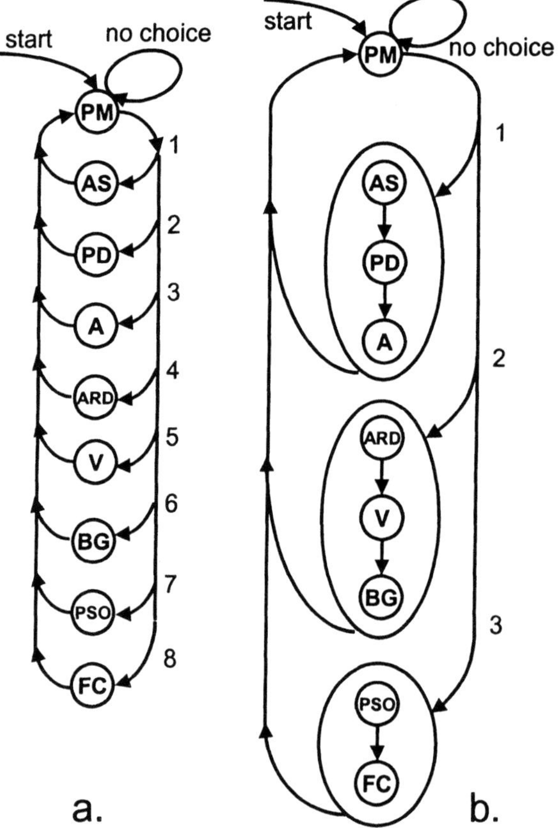

Figure 1. Each call can be described as a state machine. States are: Principal Menu (PM), Age and Sex (AS), Past Diagnoses (PD), Adverse Reactions to Drugs (ARD), Vaccinations (V), Blood Group (BG), Past Surgery Operations (PSO), Final Comment (FC). **a)** State chart representing possible flows of phone calls when each user choice brings one piece of information. **b)** As previous, but similar nodes are grouped together.

By aggregating related topics, approach (b) in Figure 1 allows speak-ER to more effectively limit the number of choices presented to the user, while delivering the same information. . After listening to a question, the user can respond by pressing one or more buttons on the telephone, or speaking the correspondent number, for example: "Press 1 to continue...", user presses 1; "Type your PIN followed by a sharp", user types 12345#; “Say your name”, the user speaks his/her name.

2.3 Prompt Access

When facing emergency conditions, health care providers should never be confronted with a queue to get information from the speak-ER system. Medical record information should be available as quickly as possible. Therefore, speak-ER system requirements must be designed to achieve the following performances in even the worst conditions:

- no more than 0.5% of calls find the system busy;
- emergency care providers calling speak-ER find it free immediately or at most within 30 seconds after the first call attempt.

According to both duration and forecast number of calls per time unit, a suitable number of telephone lines must be kept available.

2.4 Inbound and Outbound Phone Calls

In the "Inbound Calls" modality, the system will require users to give their login and password to identify themselves. In the "Outbound Calls" modality, after having received a call the system will disconnect it and immediately start an outbound call to the patient's predetermined phone number. In doing so, the addressee is identified in a more robust manner. To some extent subjecting the caller to a time consuming identification process is avoidable. Extended tests will be performed to decide which modality, between inbound and outbound calls, is more appropriate for different types of users and scenarios.

2.5 Privacy

To achieve privacy, the speak-ER system will have to perform three critical actions: identify the doctor; identify the patient; authorize this doctor to access information about this patient. For "Inbound Calls", three failed attempts to identify a user results in call termination.

2.6 Infrastructures and Tools

We chose to use the IBM Informix Dynamic Server [9] platform, since MyAngelWeb® was already developed for this platform. Moreover, an Informix trained and skilled staff was available on site, at CILEA [10] (Inter-university Consortium for the Technology of Communication and Information). As far as the Telephone Application Program Interface (TAPI) is concerned, we chose to develop the application in a Microsoft environment. Thus, we could utilize the available TAPI libraries, providing access to telephony hardware, allowing us to manage phone lines at a high abstraction layer. Additionally, this offers support for most all telephony hardware that could be in use in a production environment. With appropriate software drivers, voice modems can also be used instead of telephony hardware. We used the Text-To-Speech (TTS) system, with an Italian engine developed by Lucent Technology of Bell Labs Innovations [11]. When information is stored in plain text format, the text data are converted to an audible spoken message through a TTS engine. We chose to use this engine because a developer version is available at low cost. Because of the compatibility granted by the Microsoft Speech Application Program Interface (SAPI) platform [12], it is possible to test the system with any other SAPI compliant TTS engine.

3. Results

System testing included evaluations of the quality of the received message; the speaking durations; and the number of telephone lines required to avoid call delays.

Received message quality depends on several specific elements of two primary categories: user interaction and information sequence. End users must directly evaluate whether the presentation of an audible message by a "speaking record" is appropriate, effective, and easily understood. However, satisfactory real time user intelligibility is a necessary measure for any content presentation understanding, not just this type. Unfortunately, intelligibility can be compromised by a number of elements: imperfect pronunciation, static and noise, hearing impairment, and a attention lapse. Basic cautions include , maintaining a speech speed around 75 words/minute (it is true that, in radio news program, news is read more quickly, but spoken news messages are typically shorter and simpler than medical record messages), and keeping messages as clear and as brief as possible.

Message length can be measured by the countable length in words/syllables or by the duration in seconds. Further, it can be calculated on a single medical record, or as a mean for a group of medical records. Tables 1 and 2 summarize length and duration statistics. They describe records for 20 of the patients already enrolled in MyAngelWeb®, whose medical records have been restructured for speak-ER.

4. Discussion

For years, implementation concepts and techniques for a personal medical record effective and secure enough for use in emergency conditions have been the subject of ongoing debate and testing [13]. A frequent conceptual debate surrounds content definition. The related questions arise over the patient-based minimum data sets required to satisfy the needs of the users in the field. Operating conditions can be emergent, follow-up, research related and some others. The minimum data set issues are of perpetual interest in the ad-hoc working groups, typically active in scientific societies devoted to medical specialties [14]. Optimal solutions may require a different minimum data set for each possible condition of use yet medical records practice still lacks sufficiently granular recommendations to cover the range of need. A major reason for this absence is the relevant amount of time and effort spent preliminarily organizing the medical record content. Often, such costs are difficult to justify to health care providers, even if the end product is a medical record robust enough for other attractive uses, such as defense against malpractice accusations. Often, the return on investment is perceived to be too low, but this perception is clearly false when a patient has been hospitalized in two different institutions. In this case, it is currently likely that the two medical records, even though both in digital form, are never truly integrated into one record.

Table 1. Reading length measured in number of words for each node of speak-ER phone calls for twenty patient medical records

1 - Age
2 - Sex
3 - Diagnoses
4 - Allergies
5 - Adverse Reactions to Drugs
6 - Vaccinations
7 - Blood Group
8 - Past Surgery Operations
9 - Final Comment
10 -Total words

	1	2	3	4	5	6	7	8	9	10
Patient I	2	1	9	1	1	2	1	14	73	104
Patient II	2	1	11	9	4	1	1	9	30	68
Patient III	2	1	18	1	6	1	1	8	27	65
Patient IV	2	1	16	1	1	1	1	4	58	85
Patient V	2	1	14	2	2	2	1	8	6	38
Patient VI	2	1	10	2	2	2	2	13	9	43
Patient VII	2	1	17	1	1	1	1	30	6	60
Patient VIII	2	1	9	1	1	1	1	1	48	65
Patient IX	2	1	13	1	1	1	1	11	16	47
Patient X	2	1	17	1	1	1	1	8	50	82
Patient XI	2	1	13	1	1	1	1	11	19	50
Patient XII	2	1	13	1	1	1	2	5	18	44
Patient XIII	2	1	5	3	1	2	1	10	18	43
Patient XIV	2	1	29	1	2	7	2	1	9	54
Patient XV	2	1	8	2	2	2	6	51	0	74
Patient XVI	2	1	10	2	2	2	2	12	10	43
Patient XVII	2	1	8	2	2	2	4	0	0	21
Patient XVIII	2	1	30	2	2	2	3	0	0	42
Patient XIX	2	1	25	2	2	2	2	2	17	55
Patient XX	2	1	5	2	2	2	3	2	18	37
Min	2	1	5	1	1	1	1	0	0	21
Max	2	1	30	9	6	7	6	51	73	104
Mean	2,00	1,00	14,00	1,90	1,85	1,80	1,85	10,00	21,60	56,00

This implies that the balance of "return on investment" is negative when calculated from the provider perspective, but at the patient level the "return on investment" balance may sum differently, due to differing priorities. Of course, patients rarely have the skills or resources necessary to properly prepare and maintain their personal medical records, such that they could be used as needed. Data capture and structuring must be addressed by appropriate professionals, who can offer services suitably framed in a health care service market environment. Given access to such services, patients can calculate their own "return on investment" balance according to their own priorities, independently from the different institutions where the medical data is generated.

Table 2. Reading duration in seconds for each node of speak-ER calls for twenty patient medical records

1 - Age
2 - Sex
3 - Diagnoses
4 - Allergies
5 - Adverse Reactions to Drugs
6 - Vaccinations
7 - Blood Group
8 - Past Surgery Operations
9 - Final Comment
10 -Total Time [sec] for Reading Words
11 - Total Time [sec] for Call

	1	2	3	4	5	6	7	8	9	10	11
Patient I	1	1	7	2	2	2	2	12	36	65	173
Patient II	1	1	8	4	4	2	2	7	19	48	145
Patient III	1	1	12	2	5	2	2	7	14	46	130
Patient IV	1	1	9	2	2	2	2	8	30	57	163
Patient V	1	1	7	2	2	2	2	6	3	26	140
Patient VI	1	1	9	2	2	2	3	16	6	42	140
Patient VII	1	1	12	2	2	2	2	23	3	48	153
Patient VIII	1	1	9	2	2	2	2	0	25	44	145
Patient IX	1	1	9	2	2	2	2	8	7	34	135
Patient X	1	1	14	2	2	2	2	9	23	56	157
Patient XI	1	1	11	2	2	3	2	8	10	40	160
Patient XII	1	1	9	2	3	2	3	5	10	36	140
Patient XIII	1	1	7	2	2	2	2	7	10	34	140
Patient XIV	1	1	23	2	3	5	3	2	7	47	160
Patient XV	1	1	8	3	2	2	6	34	0	57	160
Patient XVI	1	1	4	2	2	2	3	15	8	38	140
Patient XVII	1	1	5	2	2	2	4	0	0	17	145
Patient XVIII	1	1	20	2	2	2	4	0	0	32	140
Patient XIX	1	1	16	2	2	2	2	2	5	33	130
Patient XX	1	1	5	2	2	2	4	4	11	32	140
Min	1	1	4	2	2	2	2	0	0	17	130
Max	1	1	23	4	5	5	6	34	36	65	173
Mean	1,00	1,00	10,20	2,15	2,35	2,20	2,70	8,65	11,35	41,60	146,80

Health care smart cards [15] were introduced in the health informatics field several years ago. After years of improvement, smart cards performance has improved considerably. Today, some cards embed a digital processor and their storage capacity achieves at least 128 Kilo bytes. It is debatable whether this storage capacity is of interest for health care applications [16], how much information will be stored, and what important information will be excluded. However, the major point is clear from the answer to a different question: How accessible is the information stored on a health card to health care professionals? One major hurdle is the fact that smart card readers have never become ubiquitous PC peripherals. Compact Disk (CD) readers and writers, Digital Video Disk (DVDs) readers and writers, modems, and liquid crystals displays (LCDs) are all examples of PC peripherals developed after smart card readers and writers. However, these devices are currently default peripherals for most every desktop and even laptop. Card readers and writers have never achieved this status. Thus, any storage of patient health data in a smart card will face potentially low usability due to the absence or considerable expense of necessary end user hardware.

As with any web site, health care web sites can be accessed easily from most geographic locations [17]. Any common PC with an Internet connection is sufficient to enable access. However, there are issues that need to be addressed. Prompt service must be a given. Systems responding to users by displaying a message such as "the server could be down. Try again later", is unacceptable when the health care provider is taking care of a patient in an emergency situation. Duplicate "mirror sites" for record data and high-speed connections should be properly configured and maintained. Additionally, privacy protection is an especially serious problem, since possible system intrusion by phone or Internet can occur without raising as much suspicion as it would in a physical intrusion, where the unauthorized person may appear out of place to employees in the vicinity.

Mobile phones can readily facilitate Internet access. Such phones have memory on-board and are hand held. Therefore, they combine the strengths of health smart cards with those of health web sites, as well as offering a voice channel. Mobile phones can forward health information to caregivers even when they have no time to stand in front of a computer display and read the information. Unfortunately, there are obvious problems. In reading a written message, the users read and absorb information at their own pace. When readers get "lost", they go back to read all and only what they have missed. Such "going back" does not require any action by the document or system. Conversely, in listening to a voice message the pace is determined by the delivery system, not the user. If listeners get lost, they need to rewind to the missed part of the message and play it again. Another drawback is the size of mobile phone or palm top displays: they are considerably smaller than typical displays for PCs. Nevertheless, the fact that mobile phones are already so widespread suggests a positive future for their effective use in the clinical environment.

5. Conclusions

Our speak-ER project approaches the problem of deriving a speaking medical record from one of the professionally prepared web medical record systems for patients at risk of emergency, such as MyAngelWeb® [5, 7, 8]. The major practical aim of the project is to let a personal medical presentation of a patient at risk of emergency be accessed from mobile phones by an aiding health care provider. During the project design and implementation we focused on the simplicity of the interaction and ensuring high availability. We accomplished this by using low-cost server devices.

Because of many reasons described earlier, we had to restructure MyAngelWeb® clinical records to achieve audible delivery. A major need was decreasing the number of alternatives presented, step after step, to the end user. Another need was related to shortening – and in some cases restructuring - the clinical presentations, considered too long for being acceptably received by an end user.

Future work will deal with testing the use of pre-recorded audio files instead of active voice synthesizers. This approach may improve comprehension. The use of palm top devices should also be investigated as an alternative to mobile phones.

6. Appendixes

6.1 Summary of Web-based Initiatives Offering Personal Digital Medical Record Services

In this summary seven of the most important web-based initiatives offering personal medical record services have been considered and studied.

Not all of the web sites are optimized for the availability of data in emergency situations. The scope of service is often to provide patients with an instrument to manage their own medical records and to give them the opportunity to conveniently retrieve data. Only with a few services would it be possibile for medical rescue teams to access this information in urgent conditions. Table 3 shows a comparison of these web sites :

Table 3. Comparison of web-based initiatives offering personal digital medical record services

1 - Arrange own Medical Record
2 - Arrange Family's Medical Record
3 - Personal Area
4 - Get Appointment and Receive Prescription
5 - Store Document via Fax
6 - Receive Document via Fax
7 - General Information
8 - Emergency Card
9 - Doctor Oriented for Patient Medical Record
10 - Forum and Chat
11 - Vocal Functions

	1	**2**	**3**	**4**	**5**	**6**	**7**	**8**	**9**	**10**	**11**
WebMD www.webmd.com	X	X	X	X			X	X			
AboutMyHealth www.aboutmyhealth.com	X		X	X		X					
PersonalMD www.personalmd.com	X		X		X						
WellMed www.wellmed.com	X						X	X			
DrKoop www.drkoop.com							X				
Hypercharts www.hypercharts.com									X		
MedicalRecord www.medicalrecord.com	X		X			X	X			X	
speak-ER MyAngelWeb www. MyAngelWeb.net	X							X			X

6.1.1 WebMD

After enrolling with the WebMD site [18], users have the option to organize clinical information about themselves and their family members. Users can retrieve clinical information from anywhere, anytime. After login, users have a completely customizable restricted areato store information available at their own discretion.

6.1.2 AboutMyHealth

The slogan of the AboutMyHealth service [19] is: "it is you who knows better than anyone your health state". The service allows the user to send messages to doctors in order to get appointments and receive prescriptions; users can also realize and visualize their personal health record. The main purpose is managing the medical documentation in order not to loose information and to retrieve it effectively.

6.1.3 PersonalMD

The PersonalMD service [6] allows users to store their own medical record, which can contain identifying and emergency contacts, health conditions (allergies, drugs in use), family medical history, vaccinations, and medical devices in use. It also offers the ability to insert documents in the system via fax. All data are stored as images. Moreover, it is possible to receive them by fax: the system, connected to a fax or a server, forwards the images to the number indicated by the user. PersonalMD offers also a membership card that allows doctors to receive information about their patients. This card explains the procedure to obtain via fax a copy of patients' medical documents.

6.1.4 WellMed

The WellMed service [20] allows all users enrolled in the service to receive information on their health status. There is also the option to store and manage medical information online. Moreover, this service offers a personalized Emergency Card that users can keep handy, containing the patient's medical history.

6.1.5 DrKoop

DrKoop [21] offers to users a great amount of informationto help consumers understand their health status and prescribed medical treatments. There are different types of video segments available (explaining, for example, surgical procedures or hygiene techniques). There is also a tool that verifies the interactions among several drugs in use, an archive of information on new clinical techniques, and a search engine for retrieval of clinicians.

6.1.6 HyperCharts

HyperCharts [22] is a on-line service for doctors and institutions to maintain and manage patient data. HyperCharts bills itself as a substitute for expensive traditional medical record management software . The service does not manage medical information for emergency situations.

6.1.7 Medical Records

Medical Records [22] allows users to have a personalized home page, with visualized contents concerning their health conditions. The service also lets compile a medical record describing their health background. These data can be accessed by emergency care personnel. It is possible to plan fitness activity daily caloric intake. A chat service and forum allows users to remain in contact with each other.

6.2 Summary of Present Mobile Telephony and Tomorrow Technologies and Concepts

The concept of mobile telephony is based on the subdivision of a territory into small areas, referred to as cells [24]. In every cell there is a receiver-transmitter station that manages communications with the mobile apparatuses found in that cell.

In the following subsections we discuss briefly the diffusion of mobile phones and related applications.

6.2.1 Diffusion of Mobile Phones

Statistics demonstrate that the penetration of cellular telephones is increasing rapidly [25]. At the end of 2002, in Italy there were approximately 45 million mobile telephones, approximately two for each household. At the end of 2004, forecasts predict nearly 50 million such devices [26]. According to these statistics only 2 million devices will be of the Universal Mobile Telecommunications System (UMTS). Therefore, today the possible target for an application based on mobile technology is very large [27]. As Figure 2 shows, trends suggest a strong increase.

6.2.2 Applications Involving Mobile Phones

- Although the number of users of mobile devices is high, not all the owners would be willing to utilize every type of wireless application.

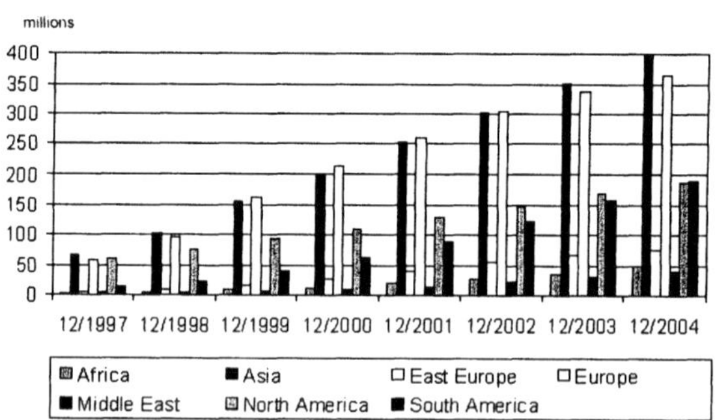

Figure 2. Spread of mobile telephony in the world. Values on vertical axis, in millions, represent the amount of subscriptions in Africa, Asia, East Europe, Europe, Middle East, North America, South America from 1997 to 2004.

6.2.2.1 WAP Applications

WAP applications have the disadvantage of small visual displays. In fact, this technology is only suitable for communicating pure textual information, due to the low navigation speed and user interaction based on the interface of a simple telephone endowed only with a numerical keyboard.

The navigation between pages is particularly frustrating for two main reasons:

- slow download of the pages;
- difficulty of moving between the miniature interfaces of a telephone WAP.

The first problem exists only where the market standard is the GSM. The first General Packet Radio Service (GPRS) telephones have reached the market in early 2004. These devices would remarkably accelerate navigation, but they are as yet little used and navigation is not cheap, dimishing the chances that they will soon be widespread. The second problem lies in the trade-off between telephone miniaturization and phone display dimensions.

7. Acknowledgements

The MyAngelWeb® project was funded in part by Assessorato alla Sanità of the Italian Lombardia Region and by the Ministero della Sanità of Italy.

References

[1] Medical Record Institute. Available at: http://www.medrecinst.com. Last access: Feb 20, 2004

[2] CORDIS. Information Society Technology. ISTweb - Home Page. Available at: http://www.cordis.lu/ist/. Last Access: Feb 20, 2004

[3] Johns ML, editor. Health information management technology. An applied approach. Chicago, IL: American Health Information Management Association; 2002.

[4] Elmasri RA, Navathe SB. Fundamentals of database systems, with e-book. 3rd ed. Reading, MA: Addison-Wesley Publishing; 2002.

[5] Pinciroli F, Nahaissi D, Boschini MJ, Ferrari R, Meloni G, Camnasio M, Camerone G. Security concept in "MyAngelWeb®", a website for the individual patient at risk of emergency. *Int J Med Inform.* 2000;60(2):203-10.

[6] PersonalMD.com - Your Lifeline Online. Available at: http://www.personalmd.com. Last Access: Feb 20, 2004

[7] Pinciroli F. MyAngelWeb®. A website for the individual patient at risk of emergency, Paper presented at the Fifth Annual Health Information Infrastructure (HII) Friends of the National Library of Medicine Conference: Science in a Digital World; 2000 Dec 4-6; Bethesda, MD, USA.

[8] Nahaissi D, Pinciroli F, Meloni G, Spaggiari P, Ferrari R. My Angel Web: organizzazione ed ingegnerizzazione del sito web del paziente a rischio d'urgenza. Milano, Italia: Franco Angeli Editore; 2000.

[9] IBM Informix Dynamic Server (IDS). Available at: http://www-306.ibm.com/software/data/informix/ids/. Last Access: Feb 20, 2004

[10] CILEA Inter-university Consortium for the Technology of Communication and Information. Available at: http://www.cilea.it. Last Access: Feb 20, 2004

[11] Bell Labs: Bell Labs Launches Web Site for Text-to-Speech Synthesis. Available at: http://www.bell labs.com/news/1997/march/5/1.html. Last Access: Feb 20, 2004

[12] Microsoft Corp. Microsoft Speech - Home. Available at: http://www.microsoft.com/speech/. Last Access: Feb 20, 2004

[13] Kim MI, Johnson KB. Personal health records: evaluation of functionality and utility. *J Am Med Inform Assoc.* 2002;9(2):171-80

[14] Harris MR, Graves JR, Solbrig HR, Elkin PL, Chute CG. Embedded structures and representation of nursing knowledge. *J Am Med Inform Assoc.* 2000;7(6):539-49

[15] Van der Broek L, Sikkel AJ, editors. Healthcards '97. Amsterdam, The Netherlands: IOS Press; 1997. (Studies in health technology and informatics; vol 49).
[16] Auber BA, Hamel G. Adoption of smart cards in the medical sector: the Canadian experience. *Soc Sci Med.* 2001;53(7):879-94.
[17] Kinzie MB, Cohn WF, Julian MF, Knaus WA. A user-centered model for web site design: needs assessment, user interface design, and rapid prototyping. *J Am Med Inform Assoc.* 2002;9(4):320-30.
[18] WebMD Corporation. WebMD -- Trustworthy, Credible, and Timely Health Information. Available at: http://www.webmd.com. Last Access: Feb 20, 2004
[19] GE Medical Systems. AboutMyHealth. Available at: http://www.aboutmyhealth.com. Last Access: Feb 20, 2004
[20] Wellmed. Available at: https://www.wellmed.com/wellmed/default.aspx. Last Access: Feb 20, 2004
[21] Drkoop.com®. Available at: http://www.drkoop.com/template.asp?ap=93. Last Access: Feb 20, 2004
[22] HyperCharts. Available at: http://www.hypercharts.com/. Last Access: Feb 20, 2004
[23] MedicalRecords. Available at: http://www.medicalrecord.com. Last Access: Feb 20, 2004
[24] Zvonar Z, Jung P, Kammerlander K, Editors. Gsm: Evolution Towards 3rd Generation Systems. Dordrecht, The Netherlands: Kluwer Academic Publishers; 2000.
[25] Mobile phone penetration. Available at: http://www.thefeature.com. Last Access: Feb 20, 2004
[26] Italia: 48,2 milioni di cellulari nel 2004. [Online 2001 Jan 23]. Available at: http://it.gsmbox.com/news/mobile_news/all/28227.gsmbox. Last Access: Feb 20, 2004
[27] Mobile phone subscriptions. Available at: http://www.thefeature.com. Last Access: Feb 20, 2004

MobiHealth: Ambulant Patient Monitoring Over Next Generation Public Wireless Networks

Aart VAN HALTEREN, Dimitri KONSTANTAS, Richard BULTS, Katarzyna WAC, Nicolai DOKOVSKY, George KOPRINKOV, Val JONES, Ing WIDYA
University of Twente, EWI/CTIT
P.O.Box 217, NL-7500 AE Enschede, The Netherlands

Abstract. The wide availability of high bandwidth public wireless networks as well as the miniaturisation of medical sensors and network access hardware allows the development of advanced ambulant patient monitoring systems. The MobiHealth project developed a complete system and service that allows the continuous monitoring of vital signals and their transmission to the health care institutes in real time using GPRS and UMTS networks. The MobiHealth system is based on the concept of a Body Area Network (BAN) allowing high personalization of the monitored signals and thus adaptation to different classes of patients. The system and service has been trialed in four European countries and for different patient cases. First results confirm the usefulness of the system and the advantages it offers to patients and medical personnel.

1 Introduction

In the next few years the expansion and availability of high bandwidth wireless networks, like GPRS and UMTS, combined with the ever-advancing miniaturization of sensor devices and computers, will give rise to new services and applications that will affect and change the daily life of citizens. An area where these new technological advances will have a major effect is health care. Citizens, being patients or non-patients, will to not only be able get medical advice from a distance but will also be able to send from any location full, detailed and accurate vital signal measurements, as if they had been taken in a medical center, implementing what we can call "ubiquitous medical care".

Towards this direction different initiatives, projects and prototypes were developed in the past few years ranging from stand-alone devices measuring and storing one specific vital sign (like insulin level) to chest bands measuring heart and blood parameters and easy to wear t-shirts with woven sensors. However all these devices are not linked with any specific service and do not provide sufficient flexibility for personalization. The device collects the vital signal data and brings to the medical expert for post-processing; no direct, on-line connection being available. On the other hand the devices that do transmit the vital signal measurements, only transmit a fixed small number of vital signals (one or two) without any possibility for expansion. Furthermore, these devices cannot be personalized, by adding for example a specialized sensor for a specific patient.

The MobiHealth project's target was to provide a solution that does not suffer from the above limitations. The project, started in May 2002 and completed in February 2004, has indeed developed a system and a service for ambulant patient monitoring over public wireless networks. Based on a body area network interconnecting different vital signal sensors and actuators, the measurements are transmitted using UMTS[1] (or GPRS) to the health care center where they are presented life to the medical personnel. This way patients can be continuously monitored and receive advice when needed. In the last months of the project 9 different trials scenarios were implemented for different types of patients. These trials allowed us to identify problems and issues in the development of mobile e-health services and identify limitations and shortcomings of the existing and forthcoming public network infrastructure.

The use of GPRS and UMTS as communication technology is essential due to the need to support a continuous connection to the healthcare center, the high bandwidth required for the transmission of the data (which can easily reach the level of 100 Kbps), the communication costs involved (in GPRS and UMTS, the cost is calculated per Kb, instead of per minute of connection) and the high quality of service required for all health related applications. These are requirements that cannot be met with current GSM technology. In fact the overall goal of MobiHealth was to evaluate the ability of 2.5 and 3G communication technologies to support innovative mobile health services. The main output of the project therefore is an assessment of the suitability of GPRS and UMTS to support such services. In addition the project delivered an architecture for, and a prototype of, a health BAN and a generic m-health service platform for provision of ubiquitous healthcare services based on Body Area Networks.

In this paper we present the developed MobiHealth system and service, give an overview of the trials performed and discuss the issues and limitations related to the deployment of 2.5/3G networks in the support of mobile health care services. Section 2 presents an overview of the different systems available today, discussing briefly their advantages and disadvantages, section 3 presents an overview of the MobiHealth architecture while section 4 describes the performed trials. Finally section 5 presents the evaluation methodology and the first results of the trials' evaluation and section 6 our conclusions and future directions.

2 Issues Related to Mobile Health Care Monitoring Systems

The need for a cost reduction in health care expenses as well as the demand from patients for ubiquitous health care provision (health care available anywhere at any time) boosted the research and the development of different types of wearable and mobile health care systems and devices. While simple vital signal measuring devices, like for example chest band for training and portable glucose control devices, have been available in the market for many years, it is only during the last few years that wearable and mobile sensors became sufficiently advanced, diverse and low cost, able to provide measurement in a quality comparable to laboratory measurements. Combined with the miniaturization of computers and communications hardware different wearable health care devices were developed and some are already available in the market.

The systems available today in the market or under development can be classified in different ways, depending on their capabilities and target use. A first element is the number of vital signal sensors that are or can be supported by the device/system. At the lower end we find specialized devices measuring only one signal, like glucose or heart rate, like the Glucowatch of Sankyo Pharma and Cygnus [2] measuring the glucose level for diabetics. In the middle we have closed systems that are able to measure a predefined set of vital signals, like the *lifeshirt* of Vivometrics [3] and VTAM from Medes [4], while at the high end we have devices that are configurable allowing the integration of an arbitrary number of sensors, like the MobiHealth system [5].

The second element to consider in a classification is the handling of the measurement data. We have from one side devices that collect the measurement data, store them locally and the user must transfer the collected measurements off-line to the health broker where they are post-processed. An important aspect is the quantity of data that can be stored, expressed in minutes or hours of measurements. On the other side we have devices and systems that transmit the data on-line, using a wireless connection, to the health broker. The important issues are the capacity (bandwidth available) of the network and the coverage area (short range in-house or use of public wireless networks).

A third element is the simplicity of use and wearability of the sensors. We have systems where the sensors are integrated in a T-shirt or a wrist watch-like device, systems where the sensors are independed devices linked wirelessly or wired to a small processing device and implantable sensors that are permanently attached to the patient.

Other issues that define the usability and functionality of an ambulant monitoring system are its autonomy, the accuracy of the measurements and the integrated medical analysis. The system autonomy depends on its power consumption (which is high for systems that transmit data using a wireless connection), while the accuracy of measurement depends on the type of sensors used (for example dry ECG sensors versus "standard" ones) and the algorithms that eliminate artefacts due to movement of the user.

3 The MobiHealth System

The MobiHealth system provides a complete end-to-end e-health platform for ambulant patient monitoring, deployed over UMTS and GPRS networks. The MobiHealth patient/user is equipped with different vital constant sensors, like blood pressure, pulse rate and ECG interconnected via the *healthcare Body Area Network* (BAN). The *Mobile Base Unit* (MBU) is the central point of the healthcare BAN, aggregating the vital sensor measurements and transmitting them via UMTS or GPRS to the back-end system, which can be located within the health broker premises or be part of a wireless service provider. From there the measurements are dispatched to the health care broker where the medical personnel monitor them. It must be noted that automated monitoring and patient feedback is currently not supported by the MobiHealth system, as this was outside the scope of the project.

3.1 The Healthcare BAN architecture

The concept of the Body Area Network originally came from IBM[6] and was developed further by many other researchers, for example at Philips [7], at the University of Twente [8], and at Fraunhofer [9]. In the Wireless World Research Forum's *Book of Visions*, we define a BAN as "*a collection of (inter) communicating devices which are worn on the body, providing an integrated set of personalised services to the user*"[10]. In the context of the MobiHealth project the *Healthcare BAN* is a health monitoring tool that consists of sensors, actuators, communication and processing facilities connected via a wireless network which is worn on the body and which moves around with the person (i.e., the BAN is the unit of roaming).

We call communication between entities within a BAN *intra-BAN communication.* To allow external communication of the BAN for remote monitoring we use a gateway, the Mobile Base Unit (MBU), which provides the *extra-BAN communication.* **Figure 1** shows the architecture of a healthcare BAN. Sensors and actuators establish an ad-hoc network and use the MBU to communicate outside the BAN. The MBU could also be implemented as a sensor or actuator that provides extra-BAN communication services.

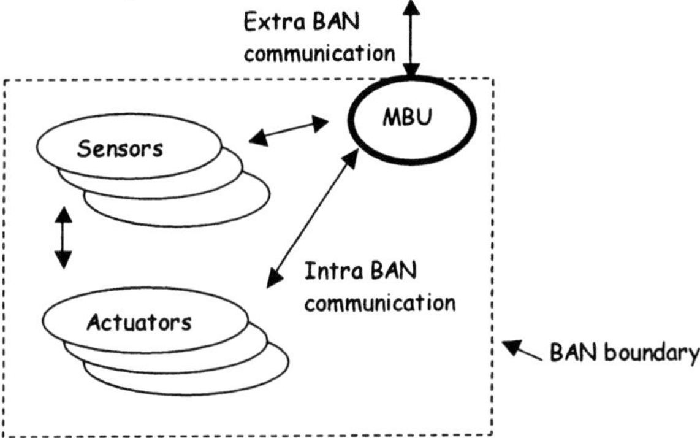

Figure 1. Healthcare BAN architecture

Intra-BAN communication is based on wireless networks like Bluetooth[11] and Zigbee[12], while the extra-BAN communications is done via GPRS and UMTS.[1]

A sensor is responsible for the data acquisition process, ensuring that a physical phenomenon, such as patient movement, muscle activity or blood flow, is first converted to an electrical signal, which is then amplified, conditioned, digitised and communicated within the BAN.

The Healthcare BAN sensors can be self-supporting and/or front-end supported. Self-supporting sensors have a power supply and facilities for amplification, conditioning, digitisation and communication. Self-supporting sensors are independent building blocks of a BAN and ensure a highly configurable healthcare BAN. However, each sensor runs at its own internal clock and may have a different sample frequency. Consequently, mechanisms for the synchronization between sensors may be needed.

Front-end supported sensors share a common power supply and data acquisition facilities. Consequently, front-end supported sensors typically operate on the same front-end clock and jointly provide multiplexed sensor samples as a single data block. This avoids the need for synchronization between sensors.

3.2 Service platform architecture

Collecting and transmitting the vital signal measurements is only part of the healthcare service developed in the MobiHealth project. The Healthcare BAN is only one part of a service platform that integrates the mobile part (healthcare BAN) and the health broker resident system. **Figure 2** shows the overall functional architecture of the MobiHealth service platform. The dotted square boxes indicate the physical location where parts of the service platform are executing. The rounded boxes represent the functional layers of the architecture. The M-health service platform consists of sensor and actuator services, intra-BAN and extra-BAN communication providers and an M-health service layer. The intra-BAN and extra-BAN communication providers represent the communication services offered by intra-BAN communication networks (e.g. Bluetooth) and extra-BAN communication networks (e.g. UMTS), respectively. The M-health service layer integrates and adds value to the intra-BAN and extra-BAN communication providers. The M-health

[1] WLAN was also used in the initial stages of the project for testing purposes.

service layer masks applications from specific characteristics of the underlying communication providers, such as the inverted consumer-producer roles.

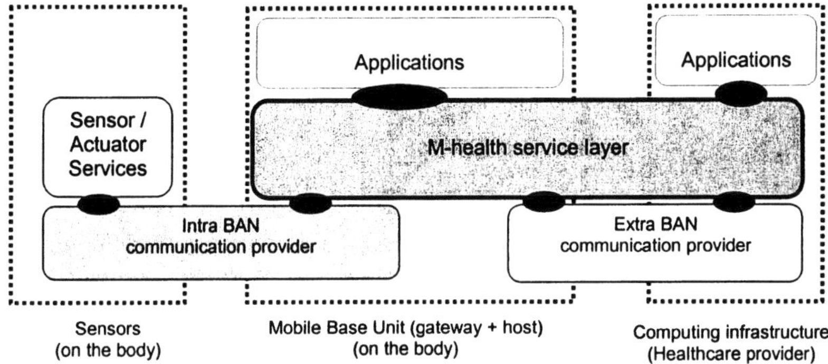

Figure 2. Service platform functional architecture

Applications that run on top of the service platform can either be deployed on the MBU (for on-site use e.g. by a visiting nurse) or on the servers or workstations of the healthcare provider, i.e. the call centre or the co-located secondary care centre in **Figure 2**. For this the M-health service platform offers a number of services including:

- *BAN registration*: the service platform maintains a list of active BANs and allows applications to retrieve the specific configuration of a BAN.
- *BAN discovery*: applications can subscribe to the platform to receive a notification in case a BAN becomes active (i.e. a patient switches on a BAN).
- *BAN authorization and authentication*: the service platform authenticates BANs and only allows authorized BANs to convey data.
- *BAN data encryption*: the platform encrypts data that is conveyed over unsecured networks
- *BAN configuration*: the service platform allows online configuration and management of the BANs, such as (de)activation of specific sensors or modification of the sample frequency of a sensor.
- *Data acquisition control*: the service platform enables applications to start, stop or temporarily interrupt the data acquisition process of a BAN.
- *Query and modify actuator status*: applications can manipulate actuators from a distance.
- *BAN data storage*: the service platform can act as an intermediate storage provider to applications. Applications determine the minimal duration of the storage.
- *BAN data monitoring*: the service platform can apply filtering algorithms on the BAN data to determine if an interesting event has taken place (e.g. a patient has dropped on the floor) and report this event to the application layer.

A refined view of the M-Health service layer is shown in **Figure 3** for the case where the M-health service platform user (e.g. at a hospital) is located remotely from the call centre. The arrows in the figure show the flow of the BAN data. The BANip entity is a protocol entity for the BAN interconnect protocol [13]. Peer entities can be found on the MBU and on the computing infrastructure (in the 'fixed' network). The BANip entities communicate through a proxy, that authenticates and authorizes the BANs' connection.

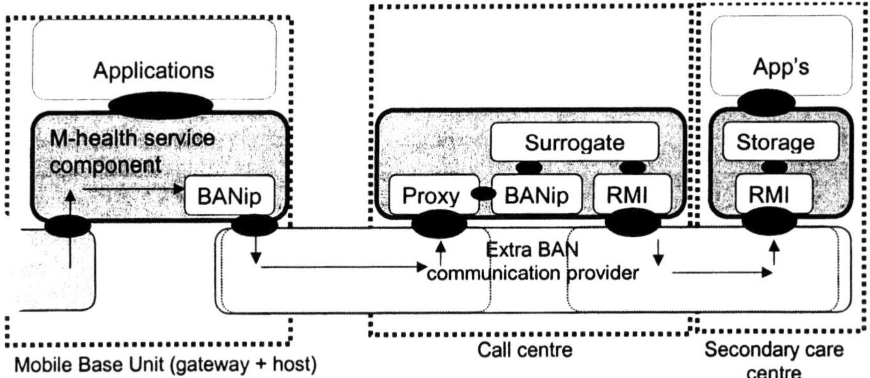

Figure 3. Refined view of the service platform

The surrogate component uses the BANip protocol to obtain BAN data. This component contains a representation of the BAN (i.e. the surrogate) and shields other components in the 'fixed' network from the BANip and direct interaction with the BAN. The surrogate component can be accessed by any application protocol, including Remote Method Invocation (RMI) as depicted in **Figure 3**. The storage entity uses RMI to interact with the surrogate as if it interacts with the remote BAN at the location of the patient, without the burden of the discovery, registration and authentication of the BANs. The surrogate component is therefore the intermediary whereto BAN data from the location of the patient is pushed and wherefrom the data is pulled by the application component residing at the secondary care centre. The storage entity provides the BAN data storage service to the application layer. Configuration, discovery and monitoring services are offered as separate entities, with the same structure as the storage entity.

Applications that use the m-health service layer can range from simple viewer applications that provide a graphical display of the BAN data, to complicated applications that analyse the data.

3.3 Service platform technical requirements

To leverage the healthcare BAN for use as a *remote* monitoring tool several issues and considerations were taken into account in the design and development of the supporting healthcare service platform. These issues reflect both commercial and social needs or restrictions, as well as technical limitations of underlying infrastructures [16]. The most important ones being *scalability*, *security* and *extra-BAN network restrictions*.

The healthcare service platform must be able to support services that cover niche healthcare cases that require the simultaneous monitoring of small numbers of patients (e.g., ranging from 10 to 100 BANs) to large-scale chronic disease management processes (e.g., 100.000+ BANs used to monitor COPD patients). In addition geographical scalability, that is global coverage, should be supported.

The healthcare service platform connects the BAN with the Internet. Consequently, the BAN is subject to attacks from malicious Internet users who either try to break into the system or frustrate its use. Therefore the healthcare service platform should be protected from attacks like Denial of Service (DoS). Mechanisms that ensure data integrity must be included to prevent corruption of BAN data. Each BAN should authenticate itself with the service platform, which should only allow authorized BANs to send BAN data.

Traditionally, providers of data (such as web servers) are deployed on a computing infrastructure with sufficient network and processing capacity. Consumers of data (such as web browsers) assume that providers are available most of the time (except for maintenance) and have sufficient bandwidth to serve a reasonable amount of consumers. This model was the one adopted by the public wireless network operators where the data consumer, i.e., the mobile device, initiates a network connection to the producer. Based on this assumption, most network operators of 2.5/3G networks hand out private space IP addresses to mobile devices. Connection establishment initiated from a fixed host on the public Internet to a mobile device is therefore inhibited.

However in the MobiHealth system each BAN *is a data producer*. For the service platform, the producer and consumer roles are thus inverted because the provider of data is deployed on a mobile device (i.e. the MBU) while the consumer of data is deployed on a fixed host with sufficient processing and communication capacity. The MBU may be temporary unavailable, due to the short life-time of batteries or because it has moved to an area without coverage of the public wireless infrastructure. The service platform therefore masks the inversion of the producer-consumer roles from the BAN and the end-users (e.g., a patient wearing the BAN or a medical specialist analyzing the BAN data).

3.4 Implementation details

The Healthcare BAN has been implemented using both front-end supported and self-supporting sensors. **Figure 4** shows the self-supporting EISlab sensor [13] (left) and a TMSI front-end (right). Both approaches use Bluetooth for intra-BAN communication. The front-end also allows ZigBee as an alternative intra-BAN communication technology. Electrodes, a movement sensor, a pulse oximeter and an alarm button are examples of sensing devices that can be attached to the front-end.

The MBU was implemented on an iPAQ H3870. This device has built-in Bluetooth capabilities and can be extended with a GPRS jacket. **Figure 5** shows a picture of the MBU that also runs a viewer application.

The BANip has been implemented using Java 2 Micro Edition (J2ME)[15]. The BANip is implemented on the MBU as an HTTP client that collects a number of samples into the payload of an HTTP POST request and invokes the post on the surrogate. We've used a standard HTTP proxy to act as a security gateway of the surrogate. In case the surrogate needs to control the MBU, these control commands are carried as payload of the HTTP reply.

The surrogate has been implemented using the Jini Surrogate architecture[16]. Jini provides the implementation for auto-discovery and registration of the BAN. In terms of the Jini architecture the surrogate is a service provider. Other components, such as the BAN data storage component, are service users from the perspective of the surrogate.

Figure 4. Self supporting sensor and a front-end

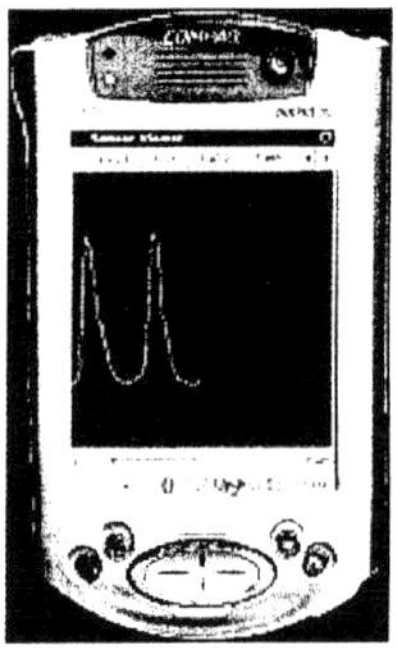

Figure 5. iPAQ H3870 acts as MBU

4 The MobiHealth Trials

The primary question addressed by the MobiHealth project was whether 2.5/3G communications technologies can support the MobiHealth vision, i.e., enable the move towards empowered managed care based on mobile health care systems. To obtain an (as much as possible) valid reply to this question, we organized and conducted nine different trials in four different countries around Europe, expecting that for some trials the existing infrastructure will be adequate while for others it may be insufficient. We must note however that the conducted trials were *not* clinical trials. The primary target of the project being the evaluation of the 2.5/3G infrastructures and *not* the validation of new medical tools and processes.

The trials also provide us the basis for a market validation of the system and service, towards further commercialisation. They are targeted at the areas of acute (trauma) care, chronic and high-risk patient monitoring and monitoring of patients in home-care settings. The trials cover a range of conditions including pregnancy, trauma, cardiology (ventricular arrhythmia), rheumatoid arthritis and respiratory insufficiency (chronic obstructive pulmonary disease), covering both use of patient BANs and health professional BANs (nurse BAN, paramedic BAN). The trials were selected to represent a range of bandwidth requirements: low (less than 12 Kbps), medium (12 – 24 Kbps) and high (greater than 24 Kbps) and to include both non-real time (like routine transmission of tri-weekly ECG) and real time requirements (e.g. alarms, transmission of vital signs in a critical trauma situation). For each application the generic MobiHealth BAN is specialized by addition of the appropriate sensor set and corresponding application software.

4.1 Trial 1 - Germany
Telemonitoring of patients with cardiac arrhythmia

The target group in this trial are patients with ventricular arrhythmia who are undergoing drug therapy. Cardiac arrhythmia is very common and in many cases is related to coronary heart disease. Around one million patients suffer from coronary heart disease in Germany today. In patients suffering from arrhythmia, ECG measurements have to be taken regularly to monitor the efficacy of drug therapy. In order to save time and reduce costs, the patient is able to transmit ECG and blood pressure via GPRS from home or elsewhere to the health call centre, where the vital signs are monitored by a cardiologist. The intention is that irregular patterns in these vital signs will be detected quickly and appropriate intervention can be initiated. This trial is to evaluate how both patients and the cardiologist gain time and cost advantages, as well as to document processes for implementation.

4.2 Trial 2 - The Netherlands
Integrated homecare for women with high-risk pregnancies

The trial will use the MobiHealth BAN to support integrated homecare for women with high-risk pregnancies. Women with high-risk pregnancies are often admitted to the hospital for longer periods of time because of possible pregnancy-related complications. Admission is necessary for the intensive monitoring of the patient and the unborn child. Homecare with continuous monitoring is desirable and can postpone hospitalisation and reduce costs, as well as offering more security for the mother and unborn child. In this trial, patients are monitored from home using the MobiHealth BAN and the (maternal and foetal) biosignals are transmitted to the hospital. An additional objective of the trial is to evaluate if such a solution postpones hospitalisation and reduces costs.

4.3 Trial 3 - The Netherlands
Tele trauma team

MobiHealth BANs will be used in trauma care both for patients and for health professionals (ambulance paramedics). The trauma patient BAN will measure vital signs which will be transmitted from the scene to the members of the trauma team located at the hospital. The paramedics wear trauma team BANs which incorporate a video camera, an audio system and a wireless communication link to the hospital. The purpose of this trial is to evaluate whether use of mobile communications can improve quality of care and decrease lag-time between the accident and the intervention. When using telemetry technology, time can be saved and thus treatment and chances for patient recovery improved. Faster intervention is expected to increase survival rates and decrease morbidity. Parameters to be measured are breathing frequency, oxygen saturation, pulse rate, blood pressure, pupil size and reactions and amount of fluids infused. Video from the scene will be transmitted assuming UMTS availability.

4.4 Trial 4 - Spain
Support of home-based healthcare services

This trial involves use of GPRS for supporting home-based care for elderly and chronically ill patients including remote assistance if needed. Patients suffer from co-morbidities including COPD. The MobiHealth nurse-BAN will be used to perform patient measurements during nurse home visits and the MobiHealth patient-BAN will be used for continuous monitoring during patient rehabilitation at home, or even outdoors. It is very important to facilitate patients' access to healthcare professionals without saturating the available resources, and this is one of main expected outcomes of the MobiHealth remote monitoring approach. Parameters to be measured are oxygen saturation, ECG, spirometry, temperature, glucose and blood pressure.

4.5 Trial 5 - Spain
Outdoor patient rehabilitation

The patients involved in this trial are chronic respiratory patients who are expected to benefit from rehabilitation programs to improve their functional status. The study aims to check the feasibility of remotely supervised outdoor training programs based on control of walking speed enabled by use of the MobiHealth BAN. The physiotherapist will receive online information on the patient's exercise performance and will provide feedback and advice. It is expected that by enabling patients to perform physical training in their own local settings, the benefits, in terms of cost and social acceptance, can be significant. Parameters to be measured are pulse oximetry, ECG and mobility with audio communication between patient and remote supervising physiotherapist.

4.6 Trial 6 - Sweden
Lighthouse alarm and locator trial

The target group involved in the trials are patients at the Lighthouse care resource centre and also clients living at home, but with the common characteristic that all have an alarm system located in their room at the Lighthouse Centre or in their home. The current system does not allow the patient any freedom related to mobility and forces the patient to be trapped at home or in their room at the Centre. By replacing the fixed alarm system with the mobile MobiHealth system the patient can move freely anywhere. In addition, positioning and vital signs are monitored and video communication is planned with UMTS .

The effectiveness of the new GPRS/UMTS-based alarm and locating device (a variant of the MobiHealth BAN) will be tested according to several determining factors: safety, convenience, empowerment of user, mobility of user and improvement in efficiency of care given.

4.7 Trial 7 - Sweden
Physical activity and impediments to activity for women with RA

Trial subjects will be women with Rheumatoid Arthritis. The use of the BAN together with the mobile communications will enable collection of a completely new kind of research data which will enhance the understanding of the difficulties and limitations which these patients face. The objective is to offer solutions that will make their lives easier.

By this collection of data, the scarce knowledge about what factors impede normal life will be supplemented and quality of life of RA patients may thereby be improved. By use of the MobiHealth BANs, the activity of the patients will be continually monitored. Parameters measured include heart rate, activity level, walking distance and stride length.

4.8 Trial 8 - Sweden
Monitoring of vital parameters in patients with respiratory insufficiency

The group of patients involved in the trial suffer from respiratory insufficiency due to chronic pulmonary diseases. These people need to be under constant medical supervision in case they suffer an aggravation of their condition. Besides needing regular check-ups, they are also dependent on oxygen therapy at home, which means oxygen delivery and close supervision. The use of the MobiHealth BANs is designed to enable the early detection of this group of diseases but also to support homecare for diagnosed patients by detecting situations where the patient requires intervention. The expected benefits are a reduction of the number of check-ups and hospitalisations needed, thus saving both time and money. Parameters measured are pulse rate, oxygen saturation and signals from a motion sensor (accelerometer).

4.9 Trial 9 - Sweden
Home care and remote consultation for recently released patients in a rural area

Home care services and the possibility of monitoring health conditions at a distance are changing the way of providing care in different situations. If suitable, home-based services are provided and patients do not need to be in hospital, for example they are recovering from an intervention. By investing in home care, hospitals have been able to significantly reduce pressure on beds and on staff time dedicated to the kind of patients named above. This trial tests transmission of clinical patient data by means of the MobiHealth BAN equipment to a physician or a registered district nurse (RDN) from patients living in a rural, low population density area. The expected benefit is that this solution will reduce the number of cases where the patient is supposed to visit a hospital for consultation unnecessarily.

5 Evaluation of the Trials

During the trials different types of data is collected in view of an evaluation of the results. The target of the evaluation is dual: first we want to verify the state of the UMTS (and GPRS) infrastructure and its suitability for mobile health applications, and second we want to explore the added value that the MobiHealth system can bring to different healthcare domains.

The evaluation of the trials will allow us to produce a set of suggestions to the wireless public network operators for the improvement, upgrade or possible modification of the infrastructure policies and mechanisms, so that applications like the ones developed in the MobiHealth project can be supported. This will be supported by concrete data indicating the (commercial) advantages that the operators will have in supporting m-health applications. Furthermore it will allow us to define a commercialisation strategy for the system and services developed, based on the capabilities of the network infrastructure, usefulness of the system and acceptance by the users.

We must note, once more, that by no means the evaluation of the trials will be done in view of a clinical evaluation of the system. A clinical evaluation is out of the scope of the project, the main target being the evaluation of the potential for m-health value added services over 2.5 and 3G communications.

At the moment of the writing of this chapter (January 2004), the trials are still ongoing and the evaluation was not yet completed. Nevertheless some preliminary results are available and will be presented in the following sections. We must however note that the results are preliminary and that they have not yet been analysed. Thus definitive conclusions cannot be (yet) drawn.

5.1 Overview of the evaluation methodology

The trials are evaluated using a methodology developed in the project and different aspects of the trials are evaluated. Specifically we evaluate the trials from the technical point of view (technical evaluation), the medical point of view (end-user and social evaluation) and from the business point of view (market evaluation).

The technical evaluation focuses on the evaluation of the performance of the communication infrastructure used in the system. The main goal being the performance evaluation of the communication infrastructure, characterized in terms of: infrastructure availability, bandwidth characteristics, percentage of data loss / corruption, transmission delay and its variation ("jitter").

The system performance related parameters are logged at the BAN side, while the generated traffic is logged by the 2.5/3G network measurement system. Logs at the BAN side declare if there were any problem regarding getting access to the network and the process of transmitting the data to the BEsys. The network log reports are used to verify if any of the logged problems at the BAN side could have been caused by the current status of the network during that time. Due to different restrictions it might not be always possible to log the network data during the trials. In this case general statistical data will be used instead.

In addition to the network performance the technical evaluation will also assess the overall system in terms of validity, accuracy and robustness of the Sensor / Actuator Service and application, the BAN and the intra-BAN communications, time delays etc.

The performance characteristics of the MobiHealth communication infrastructure are derived in two ways: objective and subjective evaluation.

The *objective evaluation* of the infrastructure includes active and passive measurements. For the active measurements an external data stream is generated (that is, we have no real MobiHealth data) and the performance characteristics of the communication paths are measured. The passive measurements will be performed in the up-and-running MobiHealth system so that real MobiHealth data are used. During the passive measurement phase, the participating operators will also perform some core-network data logging of the MobiHealth traffic characteristics.

The evaluation of the passive measurements is done in 4 steps. Step 1 involves testing on healthy volunteers in a rest state in a controlled environment (e.g., in a hospital setting) to compare the readings obtained from the BAN with readings taken from conventional equipment, and to give a first evaluation of usability, wearability, and patient satisfaction. Step 2 is like step 1 but the patients move around so that the effect of motion artefacts and wearability and functionality under more real-life circumstances can be assessed. In step 3 healthy volunteers or low risk patients are monitored in the home environment. Step 4 involves monitoring of patients in 'uncontrolled' real life situations over extended periods of time.

The *subjective evaluation* of the infrastructure's performance will be done by the end-users (healthcare professionals) who will express their perceptions of functionality and performance characteristics as experienced during the usage of the MobiHealth system.

The end user evaluation describes the usability/acceptance of the MobiHealth Services over 2.5/3G infrastructure and it will seek the subjective opinion of users regarding the new services, their usability, user interaction, satisfaction, suitability, usefulness, acceptance, independence and experiences. Also the question about the perception on the performance characteristics of the system, like: system accuracy, validity, robustness, its speed or availability of the service will be addressed by the professional users. End users in this project are defined as the patients and the health care personnel who are involved in the trials and are using the MobiHealth system. In some trials relatives and next of kin will be involved, for instance in the trial that covers homecare and remote consultation for recently released patients in a rural area.

The results of the end-user evaluation are collected using diaries, questionnaires, interviews and some objective measurements, e.g. walking distance and step-length for mobility assessments. End-users evaluation results will be compared against the performance measurements of platform to analyse existence of expected correlations. For example, the receipt of a not useful poor quality ECG, which cannot be interpreted by a professional, that coincides with large delays and packet drops in the system indicates communication throughput problems.

The goal of ***the market evaluation*** is to provide a reliable and meaningful set of criteria which will allow to make valid statements and decisions regarding the market value and potential of the MobiHealth system in the respective trial settings which are envisaged within the project. The target will be the evaluation of market, health economic and commercial potentials that describe the different factors and requirements which determine the future market success of mobile healthcare systems in general and the MobiHealth system in particular. The factors which are important and decisive in this context include: health political issues, existing market structures and processes, market players, business scenarios, value chains, potential users, users' characterization (behaviour, acceptance requirements), health economic relevance, realization of market potentials (how much and when), barriers of entry, opportunities and threats.

Nevertheless given the short duration of the project and the trials, as well as the limited number of participants and the technical limitations, it will be hard to draw sound conclusions with regard to factors like health economic relevance or users' characterization. For these cases, extrapolation will be applied as far as possible to derive some possible scenarios on potential impacts.

The evaluation criteria include elements like readiness of the healthcare system to adopt mobile services, ability to integrate respective mobile services into existing market structures and processes, and ability to meet user requirements and gain acceptance for the respective mobile services.

5.2 Some preliminary technical evaluation results

Although at the time of writing of this paper the trials are still on-going and the measurements are yet to be completed, some preliminary results regarding the performance of the UMTS and GPRS networks and technical issues related to MobiHealth BAN can be sketched. We present here some of the results from the UMTS tests and trials performed in the Netherlands using the Vodafone pre-commercial UMTS network. We must note however that the MobiHealth project is the *only* user of the Vodafone UMTS network in the Twente region. Thus we are running under the best-case environment, that is, on an empty network.

One of the first problems that we encountered in the use of the UTMS (and GPRS) networks is the *inverted producer-consumer* roles. Public networks were designed for applications where the end-user is a consumer of information, i.e, a typical user will send small requests and will receive massive data as a response. The MobiHealth system however is based on the reverse model: the end-user is the producer of information and not the consumer. The consequence of this reversal is that the network and terminal devices cannot support (in their present configuration) high bandwidth transmission emanating from the end-user. This is a limiting factor for the measurements that the MobiHealth system can send to the health broker.

To enhance portability and for being compatible with the operating systems available on portable telephones, the MobiHealth application on the MBU was programmed in Java under the CLDC Java Virtual Machine [17]. As a result we have been forced to use the HTTP protocol for transporting vital signals. However. the current HTTP protocol implementation under the CLDC Java VM does not allow for persistent HTTP connections. That means that whenever the MBU needs to send data it must establish a new TCP/IP connection. This is very expensive, in terms of performance. A better option would have been for the mobile telephones were able to use the CDC [18] platform that allows direct access to the TCP/IP layer.

A second issue related to the use of the HTTP protocol is the fact that every time a request is sent, the communication is blocked until an acknowledgment or reply is received. To solve this problem we used a technique called *chunking* [19] where multiple requests are sent without having to wait for a reply. However not all operators allow the use of chunking for their GPRS network. This eventually might cause standardization problems for services and applications that transmit continuous real time data over the GPRS and possibly UMTS

During the UMTS performance tests (active measurements) we performed tests trying to emulate a high load of the network by running 10 simultaneous UMTS transmissions. The tests (which are still on-going) indicate a performance degradation (network failure) when high bandwidth from 10 UMTS connections are simultaneously transmitted (form the same room, with each UMTS connection running from its own unique terminal). The reason for this failure is not clear yet we hope to have more data and information at the end of the tests.

On the positive side we were able to confirm the stability of the Vodafone UMTS network in the Netherlands. Tests done with a moving station (a car roaming within the Enschede coverage area) allowed us to maintain a connection of at least 64Kbps (up and down link) crossing over cell boundaries and under different speeds. The maximum bandwidth available for a fixed station of 64Kbps uplink and 384 downlink is readily available and stable thought out the coverage area (our terminal devices – Nokia UMTS telephones – do not allow us to obtain higher bandwidths).

The available data bandwidth over GPRS (and UMTS) depends on the strength of the signal at the user location. Although the GPRS and UMTS telephones do indicate the signal strength during operation, this is not the case for the PCMCIA cards integrated with the iPAQ. Some PCMCIA cards allow the control of the signal strength using proprietary software, *but only during set up*. During data transmission the signal strength information is not available. However this information is of major importance for the MobiHealth application, since it will allow us to estimate the available bandwidth and to control the data transmission rate accordingly. Currently, we have the situation that when transmitting at high bandwidth at an area with strong signal and we pass to an area where the signal is low, we are not able to lower the data transmission rate and as a result the system gets overloaded. We thus believe that the signal rate as well as the encoding schema used during the transmission should be available to the application under a standardized API for all types of GPRS/UMTS terminals, whether these terminals are PCMCIA cards or regular mobile phones.

6 Conclusions

At time of writing the MobiHealth project has been running for 20 months (since May 2002). In the rather short duration of the project a great many problems and challenges have been encountered and much progress has been made. The starting point was a vision of ubiquitous mobile health services based on Body Area Networks. During the project we have designed and prototyped a health BAN and a BAN service platform and developed services for different patient groups according to the requirements specified by the clinical partners. Patient trials have begun and evaluation data are under collection for further analysis.

MobiHealth aims to give patients a more active role in the healthcare process while at the same time healthcare payers are able to manage costs more directly. The healthcare BAN and supporting service platform is an emerging technology that promises to support this aim.

In a collaborative effort between healthcare professionals and technology experts nine trials have been defined. We expect to use these trials to evaluate the functionality and performance of the BAN and service platform. The main element of this evaluation will be an analysis of the suitability of 2.5/3G public wireless infrastructures for the support of remote healthcare monitoring. We intend to evaluate the social impact, user satisfaction and usability of the BAN on the patient and professional experience. Trials have already started and initial feedback indicates that our remote healthcare monitoring system is an important technology that facilitates the move towards empowered managed care.

MobiHealth has resulted in an early prototype of the BAN, engineered mainly by integration of existing technologies without focusing on miniaturization or optimisation of power consumption. The main focus has been on the architecture, design and implementation of an m-health service platform. The result is a first version of a service platform whose architecture is comprised of a set of clearly defined components.

It should not be thought however that all problems have been overcome even with use of current technologies. Ambulatory monitoring is more successful for some biosignals than others, for example some measurements are severely disrupted by movement artefacts. Some monitoring equipment is still too cumbersome for ambulatory use, because of the nature of the equipment or because of power requirements. In the area of wireless (tele)communication technologies (even with 2.5 and 3G) we still suffer from limited bandwidth for some applications, such as those which require serving many simultaneous users with applications requiring high bandwidth.

The use of BANs and wireless communications in personal healthcare systems still raises important challenges relating to security, integrity and privacy of data during transmission. This applies to both local transmission (eg. intra-BAN) and long range (eg. extra-BAN) communications. End-to-end security and Quality of Service guarantees need to be implemented. Safety of hardware (eg. electrical safety, emissions, interference) and reliability and correctness of applications must also be a priority in deployment of mobile services. Comfort and convenience of sensors or BANs worn long term for continuous monitoring is important for usability and user acceptance. Timeliness of information availability in the face of unreliable performance of underlying network services is another issue. Provision of seamless services across regional and national boundaries multiplies these difficulties. Powering *always on* devices and continuous transmission will continue to raise technical challenges. Business models for healthcare and accounting and billing models for network services need to evolve if technical innovations are to be exploited fully. Standardisation at all levels is essential for open solutions to prevail. At the same time specialization, customisation and personalisation are widely considered to be success criteria for innovative services.

Although our formal work in the MobiHealth project will be completed in the end of February of 2004, plans are underway for the creation of a venture for the further development and commercialisation of the results. The great interest shown by healthcare organizations and commercial companies, as well as the products that become available in the market every day and the interest shown by patients encourages us to proceed as fast as possible in the creation of a company that will promote and commercialise the MobiHealth services and platform. We expect that by the end of the 2004 to have a first version of a commercial system available to interested users in different European countries.

References

[1] UMTS Forum, http://www.umts-forum.org
[2] Sankyo Pharma and Cygnus, GlucoWatch, http://www.glucowatch.com
[3] Vivometrics, LifeShirt, http://www.vivometrics.com
[4] VTAM project, http://www.medes.fr/VTAMN.html
[5] MobiHealth project, http://www.mobihealth.org
[6] Zimmerman, T.G., 1999, 'Wireless networked devices: A new paradigm for computing and communication', *IBM Systems Journal*, Vol. 38, No 4.
[7] van Dam, K, S. Pitchers and M. Barnard, 'Body Area Networks: Towards a Wearable Future', Proc. WWRF kick off meeting, Munich, Germany, 6-7 March 2001; http://www.wireless-world-research.org/.
[8] Jones, V. M., Bults, R. A. G., Konstantas, D., Vierhout, P. A. M., 2001a, Healthcare PANs: Personal Area Networks for trauma care and home care, *Proceedings Fourth International Symposium on Wireless Personal Multimedia Communications* (WPMC), Sept. 9-12, 2001, Aalborg, Denmark, http://wpmc01.org/, ISBN 87-988568-0-4
[9] Schmidt, R., 2001, *Patients emit an aura of data*, Fraunhofer-Gesellschaft, www.fraunhofer.de/english/press/md/md2001/md11-2001_t1.html
[10] Wireless World Research Forum, 2001, *The Book of Visions 2001: Visions of the Wireless World*, Version 1.0, December 2001; http://www.wireless-world-research.org/
[11] BlueTooth, 2003; http://www.bluetooth.org/
[12] ZigBee Alliance, "IEEE 802.15.4, ZigBee standard", http://www.zigbee.org/
[13] Nikolay Dokovsky, Aart van Halteren, Ing Widya, "BANip: enabling remote healthcare monitoring with Body Area Networks", FIJI, International Workshop on scientiFic engIneering of Distributed Java applIcations, November 27-28, 2003, Luxembourg.
[14] Åke Östmark, Linus Svensson, Per Lindgren, Jerker Delsing, "Mobile Medical Applications Made Feasible Through Use of EIS Platforms", IMTC 2003 – Instrumentation and Measurement Technology Conference, Vail, CO, USA, 20-22 May 2003.
[15] Sun Microsystems, "CDC: An Application Framework for Personal Mobile Devices", June 2003, http://java.sun.com/j2me
[16] Sun Microsystems, "Jini Technology Surrogate Architecture Specification", July 2001, http://surrogate.jini.org/
[17] Sun Microsystems, Connected Limited Device Configuration (CLDC), http://java.sun.com/products/cldc/
[18] Sun Microsystems, Connected Device Configuration (CDC), http://java.sun.com/products/cdc/
[19] Sun Microsystems, HTTP chunking, http://developers.sun.com/techtopics/mobility/midp/questions/chunking/
[20] I. Widya, A. van Halteren, V. Jones, R. Bults,D. Konstantas, P. Vierhout, J. Peuscher, "Telematic Requirements for a Mobile and Wireless Healthcare System derived from Enterprise Models" in proceedings of ConTEL'03 (7th International Conference on Telecommunications), 11-13 June 2003, Zagreb, Croatia.

E-Health: Current Status and Future Trends
G. Demiris (Ed.)
IOS Press, 2004

Service Level Web Monitoring in the Field Management of Emergencies

Felice CATANIA[1], Cesare COLOMBO[2], Maurizio MARZEGALLI[3], Gabriella BORGHI[4], Francesco PINCIROLI[5]
[1]*Master in Telemedicine and Telehealth of Politecnico di Milano - Italy*
[2]*Cefriel – Politecnico di Milano – Italy*
[3]*Azienda Ospedaliera San Carlo - Milano – Italy*
[4]*Assessorato alla Sanità - Regione Lombardia – Milano - Italy*
[5]*Dipartimento di Bioingegneria – Politecnico di Milano – Italy*
also with Istituto di Ingegneria Biomedica of the Italian National Research Council and with MultiMedica Hospitals – Milano – Italy

Abstract. Cardiologic Emergency Project is based on a hospital network in Milan, Italy, in order to provide patients with more efficient first aid immediately after the occurrence of an Acute Coronary Syndrome. The Project includes ECG transmission from running ambulances to the 118 telephone central help desk, and from there to the suitable hospital. Since the maximum total transfer time should stay within a few tens of minutes, and given that a number of different factors may cause very dangerous delays, the effective coordination of several healthcare systems, devices and organizations is critical. Monitoring of the activities on each component is a must. Cardiologic Emergency Project uses a Web application devoted to the monitoring and evaluation of the service levels. Web applications allow the quantitative monitoring of the durations of extra-hospital operations. Several types of tables and graphics are automatically filled for the best care of the patient. For example, given a lengthy total time request by a satisfactory full ECG transmission, the system allows analysis of the ECG machine, of the cellular phone partial-only coverage along the ambulance pathway, of the transfer time in rush hours, etc., to determine which elements in the process can be improved to avoid future delays.

Introduction

The Cardiologic Emergency Network was created in Milan, Italy, to coordinate the activities of most of the hospitals in the city in order to deliver more efficient first aid care to Acute Coronary Syndrome (ACS) cases, such as myocardial infarctions.

For ACS patients it is fundamental to reduce any avoidable delay in the provision of the best treatment to the patient. The assistance to the patient in hospital, such as pharmacological therapies based on fibrinolitics and angioplasty operations, must be delivered as soon as possible within 1 hour after the hearth attack. However, there are two types of problems: not every cardiology ward can provide the right treatment and it requires approximately 30 minutes to prepare an operating room for angioplasty. For those reasons, it is important to execute the triage of the patient as soon as possible and to alert the cardiology ward of the destination hospital before the arrival of the patient.

The Cardiologic Emergency Service of Milan City reaches those objectives thorough a telecommunication network among hospitals, Advanced Life Support Ambulances (ALS Ambulances), and the Control Station 118 (CS-118 - similar to 911 in America) that coordinates ambulances.

The network must enable ambulances to send ECGs and vital signs to CS-118With these pieces of information, it is possible to choose the best destination hospital for the patient and to alert the cardiology ward of that hospital (with the consequent transmission of ECGs). In the period September 2000 to September 2003, 2827 ECGs were transmitted through the cardiologic emergency network.

At this time, the network needs to promote itself from an experimental phase to a consolidated and affordable phase. For this reason, the goal of the work presented in this paper is to create a Service Level Web Monitoring System able to provide tools to control the efficiency and efficacy of the emergency network. The work was conducted within the department of Telemedicine and Telehealth of Politecnico di Milano and offers supervision of different types of parameters:

- Time of extra-hospital interventions (tables and chart of the most significant parameters)
- Workloads and functionalities of devices on ambulances (tables of parameters for each device)

1. The Cardiologic Emergency Service of Milan City

1.1 Goals of the Project

The primary objectives of the Cardiologic Emergency Service of Milan City are to carry out the territorial triage of an ACS patient and to alert the cardiology ward of the destination hospital. In this way, it is possible to avoid:

- Transportation of the patient to a hospital not equipped with medical devices adequate to provide the correct treatment;
- Delay due to unnecessary exams and preparation of the operating room in the destination hospital.

To reach these goals a set of ambulances is provided with patient monitors able to measure vital signs of the patient and, in particular, to make a 12-lead ECG. In real time, they can transmit all of the data via GSM to the CS-118 allowing the right choice of the destination hospital. Finally, patient data are sent to the destination hospital to properly alert its cardiology ward.

The system follows "Guidelines 2000 for Cardiopulmonary Resuscitation and Emergency Cardiovascular Care". These guidelines propose 12-lead ECG transmissions as 1st Class solutions to treat cardiologic emergencies.

1.2 The Human and Technical Network

Seventeen cardiology wards in Milan participate in the network: beginning with 5 hospitals provided with ALS ambulances (S. Carlo Borromeo, Niguarda Ca' Granda, S. Paolo, Sacco and Fatebenefratelli), in 2001 the network expanded to maximize the efficiency of the service (Policlinico, San Raffaele, Centro Cardiologico, San Donato, and Multimedica).

As of early 2004, 7 ALS ambulances and one aid helicopter are equipped with a patient monitor and defibrillator (see Figure 1). These monitors can send ECG leads and vital signs to CS-118 via GSM. As soon as CS-118 receives patient data, it proceeds to select the best available hospital with an Intensive Cardiac Unit (ICU). The choice is based on several criteria, such as the proximity to the location of the event, the availability of beds, and so on. Patient data are then transmitted to the selected hospital (see Figure 2). Direct communication between the ambulance and the CS-118 is also possible, as needed.

Figure 1. Geographical displacement of ALS ambulances and first aid helicopter.

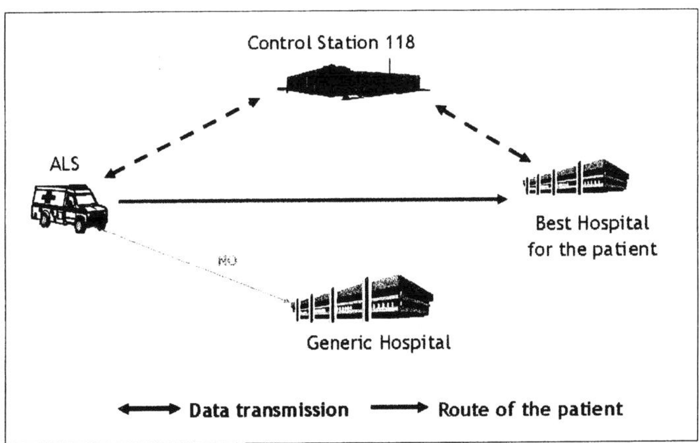

Figure 2. Interactions among ALS ambulance, CS-118, and destination hospital.

Stations for receiving data transmitted from ALS ambulances are installed in Central Station 118 and in each of the five main hospitals previously cited, enabling them to receive all available forms of patient data, from ECG to vital signs. All of the receiving stations are interconnected via phone line and are installed, depending on specific hospital needs, in the ICU, ER, or any other appropriate room. Besides receiving stations, each hospital has a set of reviewing stations connected through the hospital intranet, in order to improve system usability.

In order to include in the network also hospitals that do not have a receiving station (but are equipped for treating ACS patients), it is possible to send ECGs via fax. It is also possible to receive ECGs via fax in CS-118 from any site able to produce an ECG during a cardiologic emergency.

The devices on ALS ambulances are LIFEPAK® 12 by Medtronic. This is a biphasic patient monitor and defibrillator, with saturimeter, oscillometric noninvasive blood pressure (NIBP) monitoring, and the ability to make complete 12-lead ECGs with automatic diagnosis (see Figure 3). They are provided with a GSM card to send data. Operators can insert patient information and then send all the ECG leads, or a subset of them, to the CS-118.

Figure 3. LIFEPAK® 12 by Medtronic.

All data and events measured within a specific period stay in the device memory. These data can be transmitted together with clinical exams or downloaded at a later time.

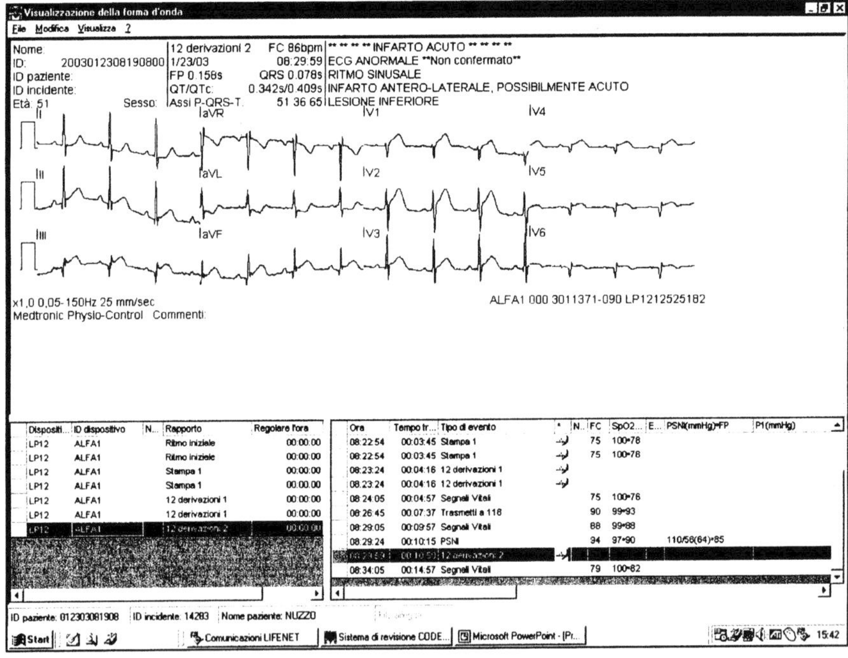

Figure 4. Screenshot of CODE-STAT™ SUITE with a 12-lead ECG, automatic diagnosis, and timing information.

The hospital and CS-118 receiving stations are dedicated PCs equipped with a receiving modem and a transmitting modem (plus audio speakers for the hospital version). Those stations are equipped with LIFENET® RS by Medtronic, which provides acoustic and visual alarms when ECGs arrive and allows the examination of leads and data transmitted by LIFEPAK® 12. LIFENET® RS archives in a database not only ECGs, but also timing information useful for analyzing the receiving process, such as time of reception, reviewing, and transmission of data.

Events recorded by LIFEPAK® 12, including measurements of vital sings and ECGs, can be analyzed after the emergency on reviewing station equipped with CODE-STAT™ SUITE (also by Medtronic) connected to the receiving station through a phone line or intranet. This software offers cardiologists the ability to insert comments and their proper diagnosis to patient cases. Its database archives all the information downloaded directly or indirectly from LIFEPAK® 12. Figure 4 shows a screenshot of the CODE-STAT™ SUITE related to a particular patient case.

1.3 Protocols and Procedures

In potential ACS cases (the need for an ACS ambulance is determined by the CS-118 operator) the clinic protocol specifies the following steps:

1. LIFEPAK® 12 Monitor must be powered on when ALS ambulance reaches the place of emergency.
2. A complete 12-lead ECG must be performed.
3. If the automatic diagnosis confirms an ACS problem, the ECG must be transmitted to CS-118. Patient monitoring must continue until the arrival at the destination hospital. If transmission fails on first attempt (e.g. in areas not covered by the GSM network), operators must continue with other attempts and alert CS-118 as soon as possible.
4. Monitor LIFEPAK® 12 must be powered off once patient is monitored by hospital medical instruments.

Timing information (like instant of power on, instant of power off and so on) is not transmitted to CS-118, but rather is downloaded directly from LIFEPAK® 12 memory.

2. Needs for a Service Monitoring

2.1 Critical Aspects of the Project

The Cardiologic Emergency Service is quite complex due to the size of the city involved (Milan has 2,900,000 inhabitants) and the consequent size of the related network of hospitals. Guaranteeing the efficiency of the network, requires a systematic management of its structural components, located in five hospitals and CS-118.

At this time, there is no centralized technical management system, with consequent drawbacks:

1. Identification and communication of problems is not always well-timed and comprehensive.
2. Time of system recovery can be very slow.

Some problems are related to hardware failure, such as a modem malfunction or a GSM card that does not send data. But it is important to consider that operators work in rotating shifts and cannot worry about problems of structural components.

Furthermore, there are critical aspects related to the organization and procedures. This requires an in-depth study on the experimentation phase to:

1. Investigate the use of resources at every step in the intervention process.
2. Improve the efficiency of the service, above all by reducing delays.

The output of this study should make possible a redefinition of procedures and processes to optimize the service.

2.2 Definition of Performance and Device Indicators

Given the above considerations, the need is clear for measurable indicators defining the appropriate service level that must be achieved to guarantee the effectiveness of the Cardiologic Emergency Service. Some indicators are collected on the basis of the real needs determined during the experimentation years. Other indicators were created to compare the opinions of physicians, network operators, and specialists from the medical device maker.

2.2.1 Performance Indicators

As mentioned, the main goal of the Cardiologic Emergency Service is to reduce the "avoidable delay". For this reason, some of the indicators are related to the time required to send ECG information over the network. In particular:

1. *POWER ON → FIRST ECG*: time between starting the emergency operation (corresponding to power on of the LIFEPAK® 12, as specified in the protocol) and the execution of the first ECG (with its diagnosis).
2. *FIRST ECG → ECG TRANSMISSION*: time between the execution of the first ECG and its transmission to the CS-118. This parameter shows delay on data transmission , critical for determining the true causes of those delays.
3. *ECG TRANSMISSION → POWER OFF*: time between the transmission of the first ECG and the arrival of the patient at the destination hospital (corresponding to power off of the LIFEPAK® 12, as specified in the protocol). This parameter shows time available for the destination hospital to prepare itself to receive the patient.
4. *POWER ON → POWER OFF*: overall assistance time from the first aid to the hospitalization (corresponding to the time between power on and power off of the patient monitor, as specified in the protocol). This parameter shows the speed of the whole assistance.

Other interesting indicators are the time needed for CS-118 to re-send ECG data to a destination hospital, and the time between receiving the ECG in a destination hospital and its medical report (see Conclusion and Future upgrades).

2.2.2 Device Indicators

The other side of the reduction of avoidable delay is that all of the network components have to work properly. This requires that all devices provided to ambulances and all of the receiving stations (both in CS-118 and in hospitals) must be ready to interoperate for ECGs transmission and reception. A set of indicators is defined to monitor devices and to assure requirements above mentioned. In particular:

- Workload and typology of interventions performed
- Number of correct and wrong transmissions for patient monitors (receptions for receiving stations)
- Date and time of the last interventions and transmissions for patient monitors (receptions for receiving stations)

3. The Service Level Web Monitoring System

3.1 Goals of the System

In this project we propose a Service Level Web Monitor System in the face of two needs: the analysis of data gathered during the years of the network experimentation and the service monitoring of the Cardiologic Emergency Service during future functioning.

In particular, it makes possible supervision on:

- Times of extra-hospital intervention, with the production of tables and graphics about trends of the more significant parameters.
- The activity of each ambulance device - functionality and number of missions - with publication of relative tables.

Times analysis can allow the detection of delays in the operation processes and it can be used in the review of working procedures of ambulances and 118 operators. Moreover, it can supply useful information for possible changes to the transmission devices setup.

The study of ambulance device data allows detection of malfunctions (i.e. the failure to transmit) and identification of wrong device setup. Moreover, the analysis of the network workload represents the monitoring of the network use and of the intervention typologies, which can supply interesting indications to determine the best size for the service.

The monitoring system is designed for centralized network management. It would find its best application in the combined use of all service databases. Nevertheless, it can be a useful instrument even in separate application on single hospital databases, in order to monitor the operation of devices working on ambulances.

Finally, it is possible and suggested to complete service level monitoring by extending the analysis to databases relative to the transmissions from CS 118 and hospitals (see 5. Conclusion and Future Upgrades). This could be useful in order to examine the course of ECGs from their creation in the ambulance, to their final destination and use.

3.2 Design and Implementation of the System

3.2.1 Functional View

At this time, network monitoring is conducted separately in the CS 118 and in the hospitals, through the analysis of data related to respective devices. Occasionally, the managers of the service in the various sites compare the results obtained from the study of their own systems.

Data extraction from these databases is not computer-based, making it hard and slow. This is the cause of long times in updating analysis. Thanks to the automation of data processing it is possible to get a continuous and systematic supervision of the service data. Network applications (LIFENET® RS, CODE-STAT™ SUITE) store data relative to the events in the respective databases.

As mentioned, the database associated with CODE-STAT™ SUITE, in the reviewing station, is populated with the data coming from the LIFEPAK® 12 monitor memory, and thus it contains the majority of data related to operations times and the work of devices that we need to analyze for the service monitoring.

The monitoring system is designed to query this database and to process its data in order to extract some possible indicators and some useful information for the management of ambulance devices (see *2.2 Definition of Performance and Device Indicators*). The examination of the results is possible thanks to tables and charts associated with selected periods of analysis.

Figure 5 shows database tables which are created by data extraction. For each emergency intervention, the software calculates the following times (described in *2.2.1 Performance Indicators)*:

1. POWER ON → FIRST ECG
2. FIRST ECG → TRANSMISSION
3. TRANSMISSION → POWER OFF
4. POWER ON → POWER OFF

Then, the web application calculates the average and the standard deviation for each value concerning the chosen analysis period.

Since TRANSMISSION and POWER OFF times are present in the database only when LIFEPAK® 12 memory is directly downloaded after the end of the intervention, and since this procedure is not yet consolidated, the application shows the percentage of cases considered in each calculation. This value is an indicator of the data completeness and reliability.

Value 4 (POWER ON → POWER OFF) is the indicator of the time needed to deliver the patient to the hospital. In order to not consider special cases related to testing of devices (powered on and immediately powered off) or related to patients who were not ultimately trnasported to the hospital (since it was not necessary), an appropriate filter was applied. It excludes cases where time 4 results less than 5 minutes.

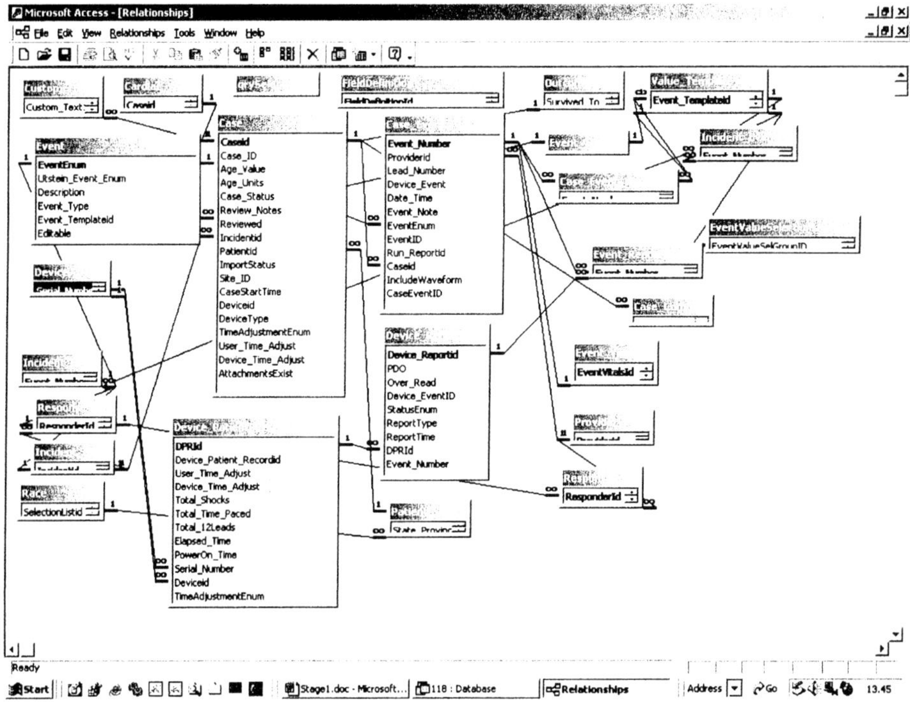

Figure 5. Tables of CODE-STAT™ SUITE database. In this Microsoft Access window, fields are created by software data extraction are shown

In order to monitor the work of LIFEPAK® 12 monitor, the software calculates the following values for each device:

- Number of POWER ON occurrences.
- Number of emergency interventions with ECG.
- Number of emergency interventions with defibrillation shock.
- Number of emergency interventions with failed transmission.
- Number of emergency interventions with correct transmission.
- Number of emergency interventions with failed transmission followed by correct transmission.
- Date of last failed transmission.
- Date of last correct transmission.
- Date of last emergency intervention with ECG.
- Date of last POWER ON.

3.2.2 Technical Details

The web application is implemented using JSP technology. It interfaces with Microsoft Access databases through the ODBC protocol. The web server used is Apache Tomcat release 4.1.12. This architecture permits use of the application via a standard Web browser, usually installed in any personal computer. In detail, for the creation and visualization of the graphics, the open source JFreeChart module was used (http://www.jfree.org/jfreechart/), which provides methods for the server side creation of various typologies of graphics and histograms. The architectural scheme designed is illustrated in the following diagram (see Figure 6).

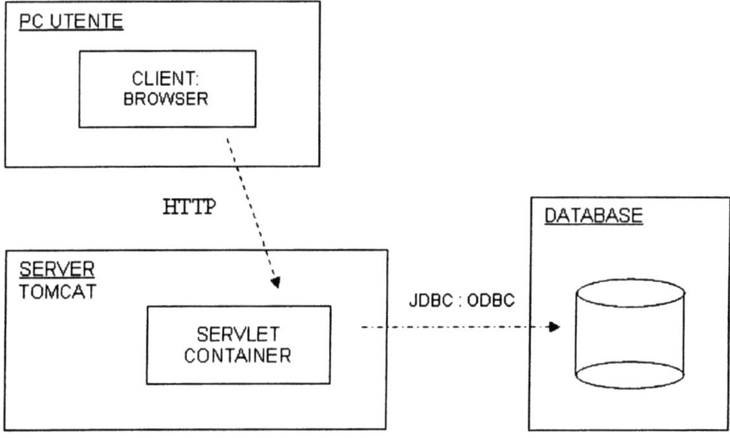

Figure 6. Deployment Diagram of the system project.

4. Results

Data were produced during three years of experimentation of the extra-hospital Cardiologic Emergency Service, from September 2000 to September 2003. The analysis of this information, relative to 2921 cases, could be an important point of reference, since the network now needs to promote itself from an experimental phase to a consolidated and affordable phase.

The monitoring system was applied to the CODE-STAT™ SUITE database of the CS 118 reviewing station, updated 1 October 2003. It contains cases sent by all LIFEPAK® 12 monitors, some of which were completed by data directly downloaded from devices and so concerns times following the transmission.

4.1 Tables and Charts of Performance Indicators

From September 2000 to September 2003, the emergency network transmitted 2827 ECGs. Table 1 shows values of the length of the emergency operations executed by LIFEPAK® 12 in ECG cases and which was chosen for the service monitoring.

Table 1. Times realized during the service experimentation, until September 2003

	POWER ON→ POWER OFF	POWER ON→ FIRST ECG	FIRST ECG→ TRANSMISSION	TRANSMISSION → POWER OFF
AVERAGE (hh:mm:ss)	00:30:03	00:05:13	00:04:53	00:15:16
STANDARD DEVIATION	00:19:54	00:05:40	00:04:20	00:16:00
% CONSIDERED CASES	3.84	75.20	13.20	0.68

Recall that in the database, cases that have been only transmitted via GSM during emergency interventions do not contain information about instances of TRANSMISSION and POWER OFF. The indicator "% CONSIDERED CASES" is the percentage of cases with complete values utilized for the respective time calculation. Nevertheless, in the transmitted cases even the POWER ON information can not be present, since the transmission can be selective and, for example, concerning only ECGs.

This is displayed Figure 7:total ECG cases (dark grey) for each month of the last year and the number (in black) of cases for which POWER ON→ FIRST ECG is calculable.

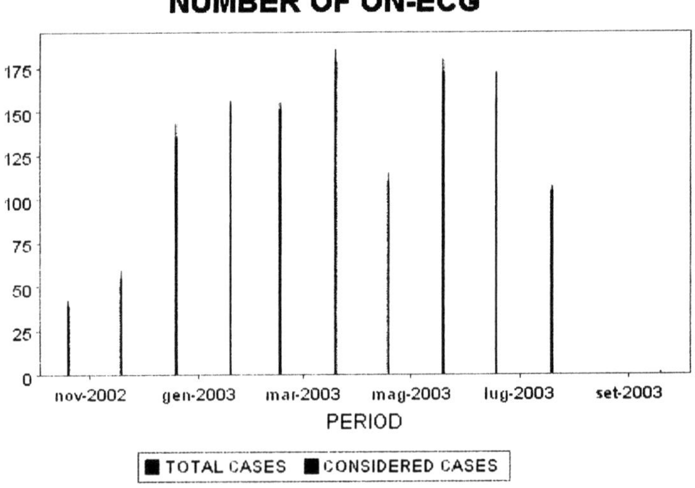

Figure 7. Trend of cases where POWER ON→FIRST ECG is computable compared to the total.

Finally, Figure 8 shows the trend of POWER ON→FIRST ECG in the last twelve months. Recall that the investigated database is updated to 1 October 2003.

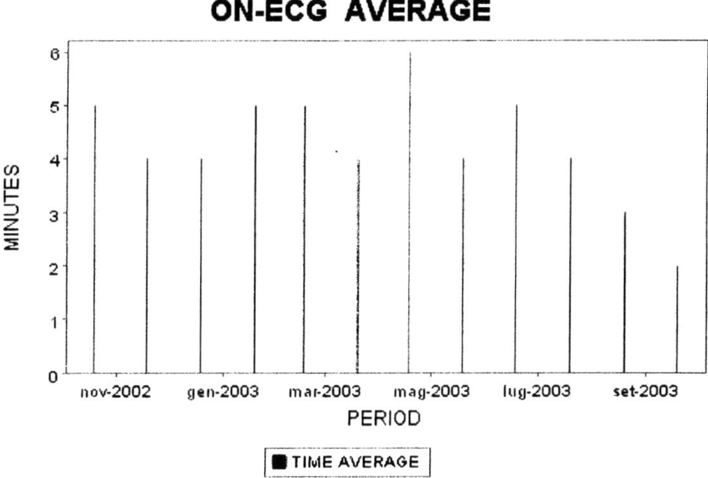

Figure 8. Trend the average value of POWER ON→FIRST ECG in the last 12 months.

Similar charts are produced for all time indicators.

4.2 Tables and Charts of Device Indicators

Table 2 shows data from LIFEPAK® 12 monitors. It demonstrates that devices were utilized not only to execute ECG, but even in interventions where patients needed a defibrillation shock. The number of shock cases is an index of the number of assisted patient who suffered from a ventricular defibrillation. In the following a brief explanation of the columns:

- Power ON: number of power on of the device.
- ECG case: number of ECG cases.
- Shock Case: number of Shock cases.
- ECG Trans OK: number of ECGs successfully transmitted.
- ECG Failed Trans: number of ECG transmissions failed.
- Trans OK After Failed: number of successful transmissions after failures.
- Last Failed Trans: date of the last failed transmission.
- Last Trans OK: date of the last successful transmission.
- Last ECG: date of the last ECG.
- Last Power On: date of the last power on.

In monitoring the work of devices it is useful to control the last operation date. Since, during the service experimentation, the transmission is a critical aspect, it is important to monitor the transmissions correctly executed and the failed ones.

Table 2. Data concerning LIFEPAK® 12 monitor functioning.

ID OF THE DEVICE ON THE VEHICLE	POWER ON	ECG CASE	SHOCK CASE	ECG: TRANS OK	ECG: FAILED TRANS	TRANS OK AFTER FAILED	LAST FAILED TRANS	LAST TRANS OK	LAST ECG	LAST POWER ON
ALFA1 LP1212525182	651	808	22	107	48	9	12:09:26 16-lug-03	14:15:58 19-lug-03	06:10:40 1-ott-03	14:29:28 20-ago-03
ALFA5FBF LP1212239811	592	673	10	118	13	1	21:36:34 23-lug-03	23:08:20 21-lug-03	11:49:48 1-ott-03	11:47:20 1-ott-03
S.PAOLO 01 LP1212939014	452	483	6	59	103	10	15:25:46 7-lug-03	19:05:34 16-lug-03	08:00:30 29-lug-03	07:57:21 29-lug-03
ALFA8SACCO LP1212261718	235	265	4	57	39	12	13:03:19 7-lug-03	16:31:48 24-lug-03	07:53:15 30-lug-03	08:07:54 30-lug-03
S CARLO 01 LP1212141506	165	208	2	30	8	0	02:58:38 1-gen-03	01:03:56 20-giu-03	20:54:27 20-lug-03	21:08:13 30-lug-03
ECHO1 LP1213073845	123	118	13	19	12	1	09:23:09 21-lug-03	07:55:45 23-lug-03	07:47:41 23-lug-03	07:43:28 23-lug-03
S.PAOLO 02 LP1212940522	7	7	0	1	0	0	NO DATA	19:18:27 23-mag-01	16:48:05 19-mar-02	16:38:46 19-mar-02
SCARLO 02 LP1212921903	4	4	0	1	2	0	21:47:45 11-lug-03	00:43:14 15-lug-03	04:01:46 15-lug-03	03:57:51 15-lug-03

4.3 First Results

Cardiologic Emergency Service managers considered the obtained results remarkable . They were able to evaluate some aspects of the service primarily on the basis of the analyzed intervals.

By the observation of the times tables, the **POWER ON→POWER OFF** value (recall that it is the indicator of the time passed from the beginning of the emergency assistance to the arrival of the patient at the hospital, as explained in *2.2.1 Performance Indicators*) appears comparable to the values obtained in similar service experimentations carried out in other metropolitan areas. Nevertheless, it is important to note that this value is here obtained for a small number of cases compared to the total.

Also the time that on average passes from monitor power on to the ECG execution (**POWER ON→ FIRST ECG**) is similar to the one measured in other experiences.

The transmission time datum (**PRIMO ECG→ TRANSMISSION**) is evidence of a crisis point in the network. The average value is too high and may require some constructive confrontations by the project managers and the 118 operators. They discover some transmission difficulties present in the Milan area, due to incomplete coverage of the GSM network.The value of the **TRANSMISSION→ POWER OFF** parameter is interesting but it is not reliable, given the small number of cases considered for its computation. This is an incentive to define the procedure of the complete download of the ambulance devices memory.

Finally, the reports concerning ambulance **devices** marked the importance of the presence of a unique network manager who has the task of investigating noteworthy evidence (i.e., the fact that, on 1 October, the majority of the last power on registrations date back to two month before).

5. Conclusions and Future Upgrades

The monitoring system of the extra-hospital Cardiologic Emergency network provides a tool for the supervision of service level indicators and of the network functioning.

Since the main goal of the Cardiologic Emergency Service is to reduce the "avoidable delay", a first set of indicators were recognized in the times of diagnosis and triage of the patients. A second set of indicators describes the network capacity of intervention by the ambulance devices functioning, workload of the monitors, their transmission functionality, and the dates of the last missions.

All these indicators can be extracted from a database which stores the ambulance devices' memory. The monitoring system queries this database and processes its data, in order to produce charts and tables that can provide the most complete data evaluation. For all time parameters, the monitoring system produces tables where average value, standard deviation, and percentage of considerable cases for calculation are illustrated. It enables investigations on all desired periods. For the supervision of the ambulance devices functioning, database queries allow computing of the indicators' values for each device, for a specified period.

The software that conducts data processing and results visualization appears easy to use, since it is designed as a Web application. The automation of the process enables continuous and systematic service supervision.

Until now, the monitoring is conducted separately in the several structures of the network. Occasionally, service managers of each structure compare results obtained by their own investigations. Data extraction from databases is manual, difficult, and time-consuming. In this context, the managing of devices is particularly problematic, since malfunctions can be identified only with considerable interaction among the different structures of the network.

The web monitoring system could be an important tool which makes real the idea of a centralized network manager that can operate on all the participating stations. The system was applied in the processing of data collected during three years of emergency network experimentation. The results confirmed that the network operates efficiently, even though the data transmission from ambulance to CS 118 should be improved.

The processed information is the object of discussion and confrontation among the service managers and the emergency operators trying to identify the positive and the problematic aspects of the system in order to start the service consolidation on the basis of these considerations.

The monitoring system can now analyze the databases of the reviewing stations of the emergency network. The natural evolution will be its extension to the analysis of data collected by the receiving stations of the CS 118 and the hospitals. In that way, we can obtain information concerning times related to data:

- To go from ambulance to CS 118.
- To be retransmitted from CS 118 to the hospital.
- To be received in the hospital.
- To be examined.

These possible analyses complete those already realized for an entire network monitoring.

References

[1] Guidelines 2000 for Cardiopulmonary Resuscitation and Emergency Cardiovascular Care. Circulation. 2000 Aug 22;102(8 Suppl):I86-9

[2] Welsh RC, Ornato J, Armstrong PW. Prehospital management of acute ST-elevation myocardial infarction: a time for reappraisal in North America. Am Heart J. 2003 Jan;145(1):1-8

[3] Luepker RV, Raczynski JM, Osganian S, Goldberg RJ, Finnegan JR Jr, Hedges JR, et al. Effect of a community intervention on patient delay and emergency medical service use in acute coronary heart disease: the Rapid Early Action for Coronary Treatment (REACT) trial. JAMA 2000;284:60-7

E-Health: Current Status and Future Trends
G. Demiris (Ed.)
IOS Press, 2004

E-Health in the Scandinavian Countries

History, Status and Future

Claus DUEDAL PEDERSEN
MedCom, Denmark

Abstract. For more than 10 years the Scandinavian countries have been focusing on utilizing information technology to increase efficiency in the delivery of healthcare services. Over the last 3 years all three countries have built closed secure IP-based healthcare networks that cover nearly all aspects of the national healthcare sector. The next step is to connect the national networks and integrate them into one large Scandinavian healthcare network. This paper describes the history of e-health in the Scandinavian Countries, the challenges and emerging trends.

Introduction

The three Scandinavian countries Norway, Sweden and Denmark, have for many years been placing emphasis on developing and improving their healthcare sector and have been examining ways to deliver healthcare services to citizens in a more efficient manner. The common characteristics of the healthcare services in these three countries are:

- equal and free (or nearly free) access to healthcare services for all citizens
- healthcare services financed by taxation
- health care institutions that are being owned and managed by public authorities; andhealthcare expenses that cover about 8-9 % of the Gross National Product (GNP)

The healthcare sectors in these three countries will also face the same challenges in the next decade. It is quiet clear that it is no longer possible to increase taxes to cover the rising cost of healthcare. There will be a significant change in the population, as the ratio of employed citizens to retired workers will drop over the next ten to twenty years from 4 :1 to 2.5 : 1. All three countries face a lack of expert health care professionals; about one third of all specialists will retire within the next five to ten years. New and in many cases costly treatment procedures are introduced by the medical industry or by clinical experts on an ongoing basis. Patients become more informed and able to access a plethora of information via the Internet, mass media and other organisations. In order to address these challenges, the Scandinavian countries have for the last ten years focused on the possibilities and benefits of the use of information technology (IT) in the health care sector. The objective in Denmark, Sweden and Norway has been to create a seamless health care delivery system for the citizens, but the specific strategies have been slightly different in the three countries. In Norway, the focus has been on development of telemedicine solutions. Sweden has been building secure networks and Denmark has implemented large-scale use of EDI-messages in the entire health care sector. Nevertheless, the three countries have been working in the same direction over the last few years, by building secure closed Internet based networks for health care professionals.

Over the last four years, there has been an informal but close cooperation between the organizations in the three countries that are responsible for the National Healthcare networks[1]. This cooperation has been very useful in making clear that there is great potential in the connection of the health networks and developing common solutions on a Scandinavian level.

Status of the eHealth in the Nordic countries

National Healthcare Networks are the backbone of the electronic communication in Denmark, Sweden and Norway. The three national networks have facilitated extensive communication between different healthcare providers of the three countries. This is illustrated in Table 1 below, which describes the current use of the three national health data networks.

Table 1. Use of national health data networks in Denmark, Sweden and Norway. How many users of electronic communication today?

	Number			Percent connected to net		
	Denmark	Sweden	Norway	Denmark	Sweden	Norway
Hospitals	70	70	62	100	100	100
Pharmacies	332	900	Few[1]	100	100	0
General practitioners	1946	4500	713[2]	89	90	40
Private specialists	453	300	n.a.	58	30	n.a.

1) Very few of the 500 pharmacies can handle prescriptions in an electronic format.
2) The number of General practitioners connected to the Norwegian health network.

In Denmark, all hospitals and pharmacies are connected to the Danish healthcare network. Additionally, 89 percent of the General Practitioners (GPs) and 58 percent of private specialists are connected to this network. It is important to stress that the connection in all cases exists under commercial conditions. Today 60 to 75 percent of the communication between the above-mentioned actors in healthcare occurs through the Danish healthcare network. In Sweden the situation is similar. All hospitals and pharmacies are part of the Swedish network. Also, the great majority (90%) of the GPs are connected to the network, while only 30% of the private specialists are connected. Although all Norwegian hospitals are connected within one network, the Norwegian healthcare network is not utilized to the same degree as the Danish and Swedish ones. Due to legal obstacles in Norway, prescriptions cannot be sent electronically and therefore, pharmacies are not connected to the network. Only 40% of the general practitioners in Norway have access to the Norwegian network.

In the following, we will discuss the infrastructure and e-health applications for each of the three Scandinavian countries.

Sweden

Infrastructure

Sjunet is a secure national network connecting Sweden's 80 public hospitals, approximately 800 primary care centres, all 900 pharmacies and a number of private institutions. Today, all of the county councils in Sweden are connected to Sjunet, and work has now started to connect the first local authorities as well.

[1] In Sweden Carelink (www.carelink.se) in Norway KITH (www.kith.no) and in Denmark MedCom (www.medcom.dk)

The infrastructure behind Sjunet is made up of an IP-based network solution built on Ethernet VLAN-technology.

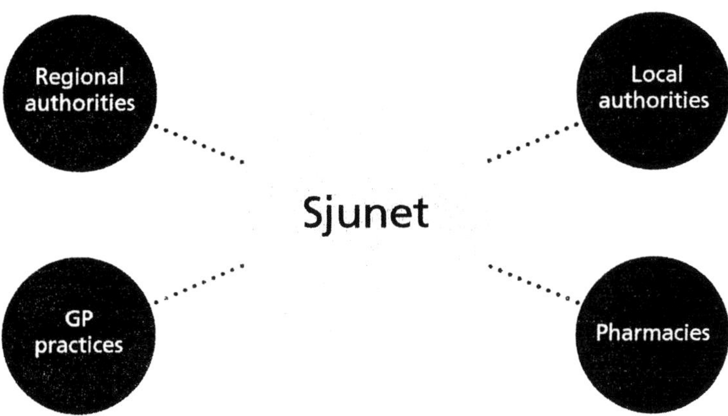

Figure 1. The infrastructure of Sjunet in Sweden

The network is a fibre-optical network, separate from the Internet. This enables a secure and reliable exchange of confidential data, such as patient records, that is not suitable for transfer over the Internet. The infrastructure is owned and managed by the Nordic Data and Telecom Operator Song Networks, which is also responsible for the support of the network.

The network manages capacities up to 1 Gbit/s, which means that it can easily handle advanced real-time critical applications. As it is based on IP, the solution is well prepared for future developments. The network is built in a ring structure, which guarantees alternative routes in the event of cable breakdown. For Sjunet, this means reliable transmission for teleradiology, videoconferences, file transfers and electronic prescriptions. Technical description can be found at www.carelink.se

Services

Examples of services currently offered by Sjunet or planned, include:
- Conference Platform for Video
- Certification Authority (CA server)
- Health Service Address (HSA) Directory
- Population Database
- Agency Node (SHS)

Most county councils in Sweden currently have a video infrastructure that serves various functions, for example video conferencing, video discussions, education and health services' planning among the various local authorities and county councils.

Applications

Several examples of Sjunet's services can be found within the field of telemedicine, including the secure transmission of patient information, clinical rounds, teleradiology and collaboration between hospitals.

Another example is the vast number of medical prescriptions that nowadays are being transmitted electronically to pharmacies. In addition, Sjunet is also used for IP telephony, file and media transmissions and access to knowledge databases. Several other interesting projects are ongoing. For example, pilot work is being carried out for the development of a node for communication with governmental agencies.

Norway

National Health net

The National Health net comprises the three lower levels of the model shown on Figure 2.

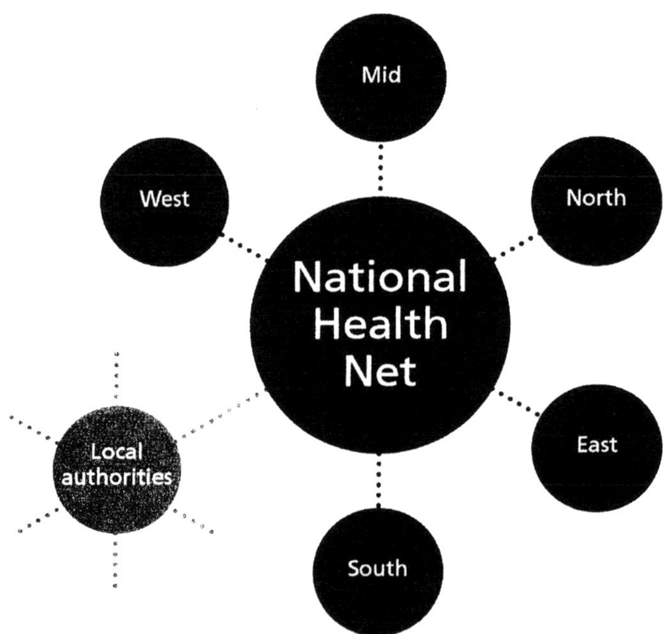

Figure 2. National Health Net

Hence, the National Health Net represents a high capacity and secure infrastructure for electronic cooperation and telemedicine consultations between the different providers of health and social services.

During the first phase, the National Health Net was implemented as a connection of five regional nets (North, Mid, West, South, East), and mainly covering the health service providers (not social care). The national connection net is owned by the Directorate of Health and Social Affairs, and the five regional nets by the respective regional health enterprises. The implementation status for the five regional nets is varying, but in progress in all regions. North and Mid regional nets are nearly fully implemented and in operation, while the other regions will achieve this status in the end of 2004. The national connection net has been in operation since August 2003.

A full integration of the six nets (five regional and national connection) is foreseen, as well as communication with the social care sector (responsibility of local authorities) through connections between National Health net and the nets for the local authorities.

Systems application

Practically, all General Practitioners have Electronic Patient Records systems (EPRs). Three out of four of all hospitals have EPR, the remaining ones will have such a system within the next two years. Two out of three of all hospitals have a Picture Archiving and Communication System (PACS) allowing for digital imaging, and all hospitals will have a PACS system within the next three years. A vast majority of local authorities have implemented IT documentation systems for the care sector.

By the end of 2004 a full implementation of the National Health Net accesible to all hospitals and GPs in Norway will have taken place. An infrastructure for secure messaging (PKI) is established. The first pilot user is the Norwegian Social Security Agency. Several telemedicine pilots are currently being carried out. Future projects include the creation of a technical infrastructure that will link the health and social sectors.

Denmark

Infrastructure

The technical infrastructure of the Danish health data net builds on connecting the existing secure networks within a closed network by using Virtual Private Network (VPN) tunnels that meet at one central intersection. The network is illustrated on Figure 3. The Danish Healthcare Network connects all 15 regional health care authorities[2], pharmacies, local authorities, private laboratories and the vast majority (89 %) of the general practitioners. At the central note, an identification system has been established, which enables persons responsible for a network to ensure that access is only possible to and from specified IP numbers. Finally, the individual user is registered with a unique user ID and password by the organizations that make traceable patient data available. This mechanism meets the activity log requirements, which are stipulated by law. A technical description is available at: www.MedCom.dk

[2] The 14 Danish counties and the Copenhagen Hospital community (Hovedstadens Sygehusfællesskab).

Figure 3. The Danish Healthcare Network

Services

The following services are currently available on the Danish health-sector data net:

- Current EDIFACT and XML communications totalling approximately 2.5 million messages per month in the Danish health sector, distributed across all significant communication streams such as prescriptions from GPs to pharmacies, discharge documents from hospitals to GPs, laboratory replies from laboratories to GPs, advice of hospital admittance from hospitals to municipal home care services, etc.
- Four counties offer web access to X-rays and descriptions and pictures from other hospitals and GPs.
- Four counties and a private laboratory offer access to laboratory data.
- Six counties have teleconsultations between dermatologists and GPs.
- A national web-based requisition server has been established, enabling GPs to order clinical chemical tests at all laboratories in the country.
- All hospitals report to a national quality database (NIP), which includes the following groups: acute gastrointestinal surgery, apoplexy, heart failure, acetabular fractures, lung cancer and schizophrenia.
- Six counties offer access to patient record data
- Videoconference services

Applications

An IT-Collaboration server that was developed in the PICNIC (IST-1999-10345) project is currently being installed in the health-sector data net. This server is a project tool to enable interorganizational patient-related communications throughout the health sector. See: www.medcom.dk/picnic/deliverables/default.htm

The future Nordic Healthcare Data Network

When examining the status of information technology (IT) integration in the health care sector of the Scandinavian countries, it becomes clear that the large scope of communication between different healthcare providers in Scandinavia is rather unique when compared to other European regions. At the same time, the three national networks are technically very similar in their infrastructure and this fact provides an exceptional opportunity to connect the three national health data networks and thereby, establish an even larger market for eHealth services in the region. The connected networks will constitute the technical infrastructure for this market.

The technical approach for the integration of the three national networks has been determined and is ready to be implemented in 2004. In addition to the Scandinavian network, a Service Portal will be established to make the potential services accessible in a user-friendly way both for users and internal/external providers. The Service Portal will be a basic business platform consisting of a web-portal and an organisational body dealing with technological and security issues, rules for being on the net, future development etc. Once the Scandinavian network is established, it can be extended to other regions or implemented at a pan-European level.

Author Index